DISLOCATION 错位

BORN IN CHINA, LIVING IN AMERICA

LYNN ZHENG

Translated by
ALEX WANG

CONTENTS 目录

一场暴雪	1
A Blizzard	9
结	19
The Knot	29
国家福利	41
National Welfare	51
缺席	65
The Absence	75
夜宿	89
One-Night Stay	99
小祖宗	111
A Little Devil	123
错位	137
Dislocation	149
异乡	163
A Strange Land	173
About the Author 关于作者	187

一场暴雪

早晨八点,刚刚亮起来的天又暗了下来。乌云从北向南慢慢地压了过来。窗外已经开始飘起了雪花,时不时还有一些冰霰敲打在窗子玻璃上。

太太正在厨房里做早饭。自从我的肝病恶化以后,每天她都要把清淡、营养的早餐送到我的面前。

"你的动作可能要快一点;外面已经开始飘雪花了。"她端着刚做好的青菜蛋花粥走了进来。"我先把你送到医院再去店里上班,差不多两小时后再去接你。如果你提前结束了,就打个电话给我。我让奥拉替我一下。"奥拉是她店里的同事。一个挺不错的美国姑娘。

"还是我自己开车去吧。"我撑起身子穿上大衣。

"算了,外面要下雪了。"她说。

我拧不过她。

九点钟,我要去见巴德医生。他是我们这个市医院里最好的肝脏科医生。这两年,我一直在他那儿就诊。

一个星期前，他的护士打电话约我今天上午去见他，说是要讨论下一步的治疗方案。医生约病人好像不多见。

巴德医生是一个略显微胖的矮个子中年男人。深蓝色的衬衫配上一条浅黄色的条纹领带，外面罩着一件合体的医院白制服。深棕色的头发梳得一丝不乱，再加上一副浅棕色的眼镜。他是我在电影里看到的那种典型的美国医生。

进门后，他和我握了握了手直接了当地说："我们仔细地研究了你的病情。你需要换肝。"

"换肝？"我竭力控制住自己的声调。这是我想都没想过的方案。

"是的，如果可能的话。这是我们目前想到的最好方案，也是我们能做的最后一步。"他毫不避讳地说。"如果不换肝，还真的不知道有什么别的办法。"巴德医生扶了扶眼镜，从架子上取下一叠表格，"用羊肝儿、猪肝儿也只是停留在医学的幻想中。"他停了一下，"你要做好思想准备，我们的肝源很紧张。队排得很长。什么时候有合适你的肝源我们不能保证，完全不能保证。"

他把带有四个轮子的圆形无背椅，轻轻地滑到我的身边坐了下来。

"不过你要打起精神，要给自己希望。"他说着，拍了拍我的肩膀。"我会为你祈祷的。"他用笔钩了一些需要检查的项目，并告诉我，我身体情况的大部分资料他们都有了，只是还要做一些换肝前的指定检查。一但有合适的肝源，又排到我了，就立刻通知我。最后他郑重地告诉我："你知道，换肝是按先来后到排队的，不管你是什么人，有再多的钱，再高的地位，我们都不设优先级。"

"知道。"我无力地点点头。

我完全不记得我是怎么做完那一项项检查的，只记得一个金发姑娘领着我从一间房间走到另一间房间，从一个和蔼的面孔换到另一个和蔼的面孔。中间太太打电话过来，我好像也没接。我不知道说什么。告诉她我要换肝又没有肝源？

狂风夹着冰霰横着砸了过来。无数颗冰粒子在半透明的冰面上滚动。天地好像翻转了九十度，一切都笼罩在苍茫之中。如果用倾盆来形容暴雨，真不知道用什么来形容这场雪。

医院的候诊大厅里挤满了人。大家无助地望着外面发呆。我在候诊大厅的一个角落坐了下来，透过走廊尽头的落地玻璃窗直直地向远处望去，心情像乌云一样凝重。

巴德医生告诉我，我的肝脏恶化程度比他们预计得要快，希望能在两个月内换肝。这就意味着，如果在两个月内没有合适我的肝源，我就没有救了。也就是说我被判了死刑，缓期两个月执行。

我闭上眼睛，努力地用理性去控制慌乱的心情。

想起两个月前的那天早晨，我用了双倍时间才把车开到公司门口，浑身上下都汗透了。车窗外所有的景物像漂了起来一样；从收音机里出来的音乐也慢得出奇，似乎每个音符都不在调子上。我努力地想把车停在车位上，可是尝试了几次都失败了。我在车里坐了好一会，想再试一次，但确切地说，我已经精疲力尽了。

公司的保安敲了敲我的车窗说:"先生,你还好吗?我们已经注意你有一会儿了。"

他弯下腰来凑近我的车窗问:"你的脸色很不好。要不要去看医生?"

我无力地摇摇头:"不用了,谢谢!"

上午有一个急需要完成的实验;下午还要给上面做一个报告。再说我不想老是缺勤,让公司的头知道我又病了。我的一生就像在不停地爬梯子。当我在向上攀登的时候,梯子似乎不断地在延升,永远不会完结。可是我真的感到爬不动了,太累了!仅仅活着就用尽了所有的力气。

"谢谢!"我用几乎听不见的声音向还站在我车窗边的保安说,"我可能休息一会儿就会好的。"

最后他们还是把我送进了医院,因为没过多久我就昏迷过去了。也就是说,从那天起我知道我的肝病开始恶化。

今年的天气真是有些反常。美国南部的冬天也会这么冷。上个月,一场持续了二十个小时的大雨,淹掉了城市里约一半的房子。到现在人们还都惊魂未定。

记得上个星期在电话里还和在西海岸上大学的儿子聊天气。我说:"全球变暖的理论要改写。"

他说:"亏你还是学技术出身的,连天气和气候都没弄明白。"

我说:"我学的技术不包括老天。"

儿子仔细解释:全球变暖后,北极的升温融化了那儿的部分冰川,搅动了原本稳定的冷气团,使得长驱直下的冷气流一直到达美国的最南部。

全球变暖和我还有关系吗?只给我两个月的时间呀!排在我前面的都有谁?我不知道。肯定有不少。我的脑子很乱。人生就像弯延曲折的冰川；不到最后一天，你真的不知道流到了哪里。在生命即将溃败的时候，我真的没有准备好。我害怕起来，感到心脏似乎要挤出喉咙。

风渐渐地弱了。大朵大朵的雪花从空中静悄悄地压了下来，短短的时间里，树木，房屋和道路就积满了厚厚的雪。来医院的人都被困在了这里。路上没有多少车在走动，除了那些不要命的。医院大厅里高挂着的电视屏幕上正在直播着天气形势，各种彩色的云图在上面翻滚着。

我拿出手机，想告诉太太这边已经结束了。当手机屏上跳出号码时，我又迅速地按掉了它。真是见鬼！都不知道我在干什么。这种鬼天气能出门吗？

一个憔悴的老年妇人走了过来，她把老人助步车放在我的座位边上，在隔着的另一个座位上坐了下来。她嘴里一边嘟嘟囔囔地说着什么，一边整理手上各种表格，然后隔着座位告诉我，这种天气几十年都没遇见了。我只是朝她略微地点点头表示赞同。此刻，我只想安静一会儿，仔细理一理纷乱的脑子。

大厅里播放着舒缓的乐曲，里面混合着各种嘈杂的声音。一阵困意袭来，我感到了一种前所未有的轻松。当一个人放下了他一直都以为是责任的东西，生命中还有什么可操心的？

手术室里，我静静地躺在手术台上。医生们的脸在我的头顶上晃动。一个长着满脸白胡子的主刀医生微笑着告诉我：你坏掉的肝脏已经取出来了，但好的还没有找到。大约要等两个月。你在这里安心地躺着，我们两个月以后再见。说完，头顶上的无影灯慢慢地暗了下来。随着手术刀和剪子的碰撞声消失后，是一声轻轻的关门声。我大声呼喊，不！不！别离开我！回应我的只是身子下边滴达、滴达的流血声……

远处，隐隐约约传来轰隆隆的声音，渐渐地越来越响。当我迷迷糊糊地睁开眼时，一架直升飞机已经接近了我的头顶上方。巨大的声音震耳欲聋，从地面上扇起的雪片四处飞散。这突如其来的景像让我恐惧；一时摸不清到底发生了什么。我的胸口又被狠狠地挤了一下。当我定下神来看清了周围的一切，才搞明白这里还是医院。那是一架急救直升机，正试着降落在大楼边上被大雪覆盖的草坪上。

直升机巨大的扇叶下有个人被抬了出来，很快被送到了对面的急救中心。一切又恢复了平静。雪仍在默默地下着……

时间一点一点地过去了，雪还没有要停的样子。中间太太打来了电话。我没有告诉她我需要换肝，不想让她为我操心。生活在异国他乡这么多年，每一步都走得不容易。

候诊大厅的那一头，我看见那位几个小时前领着我去做检查的金发姑娘。她正在来回走动着，好像在寻找什么人。

就在这时，医院的广播响了起来："陈先生，立昆陈，巴德医生在找你。请立刻到巴德医生的办公室去。立昆陈，巴德医生……"第二遍的声音显然露出了焦急。当第三遍刚出声时，我一下意识到这是在叫我。我的名字是陈立群。在美国，名总是在前，姓放在后面。他们显然把我名字中的"群"发成了"昆"。其实我很早就想起个常用的美国名字，叫个彼得，杰克什么的，但是总觉得特别别扭，所以一直拖着没有起。

我倏地站了起来，抓起大衣，迎面正碰上匆匆赶来的那个金发姑娘。她急促地对我说："我们都在找你。跟我来！"

很远就能看见巴德医生站在他的办公室门口。

"太好了！我就猜到你还在这儿。"他迎了上来，用劲地和我握了握手，虽然几个小时前我们已经握过一次。

"抓紧时间，立刻准备手术。"他看着我，非常肯定地一字一句地说。

我瞪大了眼睛，满腹疑虑地望着他。

"刚才有个出车祸的年青人没有被救过来。这该死的天气！"他用手捶了一下桌子继续说，"他是一个器官自愿捐赠者。正巧他的所有指标都适合你。"这时巴德医生的语气从悲哀转成兴奋。"所有排在你前面的患者，都被这冰雪堵在了家里。我们估计你也一定被滞溜在这里。"

这次我真的被送上了手术台。

……当麻药缓缓地流过我的身体时，我的眼前出现了天地相连的白色大海。海浪是那么柔和。我慢慢地走了进去，瞬间被白色的浪花托起，就像睡在摇篮里的婴儿。我闭上了眼睛。浪花一上一下，每次下去又被托了回来。最后一次，当浪花再一次把我往回托时，海水开始落潮，我感到整个身子一个劲地往下沉。此刻，雪白的海水在我四周旋转，太阳在海水的反射中炫得人睁不开眼。我伸出两只胳膊去遮挡太阳,突然,两只手被抓住了。

"他醒了!"

我睁开了眼睛。一个年轻的女护士正按着我的手臂。

我的手背上插着管子。输液的药瓶悬挂在架子上,一台显示心跳波形的仪器发出单调的声音。床尾,穿着淡蓝色无菌长衫的太太正微笑地看着我。从她的脸上,我看到了久违的轻松。

我的两眼湿润了。

泪,可以与我共同承担心里的痛苦和快乐。

这些年,出差、加班、熬夜和工作上各种难以承受的压力,让我的身心一直在超负荷地运行。焦虑和抑郁也轮番来访过。想想也真对不起自己。疾病就像我们叛逆的孩子,是我们没有给身体足够的关爱才让它叛逆的呀!如果不把它逼到绝路上,或许不会像今天这样。

我要善待自己,善待这个新来的伙伴。

我还要去见这个捐赠者的父母,告诉他们我是多么难过又是多么幸运。如果他们愿意,我可以做他们的儿子,还要把我的全家介绍给他们。我想了很多能为他们做的事情。

第二天,下了一天一夜的大雪终于停了。在明澈的天空下,一切显得格外清晰。

在这非同寻常的偶然事件中,让我真正地体验到了活着的感觉。活着真好!

门开了。外面是医生和护士匆匆而过的身影。我突然觉得是这么地喜欢这里,喜欢这里的一切!

A BLIZZARD

∼

Eight o'clock in the morning, and the sky that had just lit up was dark again. The black clouds slowly pressed from north to south. Snowflakes showed up outside the window, and every so often, some sleet hit the windowpane.

My wife was making breakfast in the kitchen. Since my liver disease had worsened, she had prepared a light and nutritious meal for me every morning.

"You may need to hurry; there are already snowflakes outside." She came in with the steaming egg congee. "I'll take you to the hospital before work and pick you up in about two hours. If you finish early, call me. Jasmine can cover for me." Jasmine was an associate in her store. A sweet American young lady.

"I can drive myself." I propped myself up and put on my jacket.

"Well, it's about to snow," she said.

I couldn't challenge her.

I would see Dr. Bard at 9 a.m. He was the best hepatologist in our municipal hospital. I had been seeing him for the past two years. One week ago, his nurse had called me about meeting him this morning to discuss the next-phase treatment. It seemed uncommon for a specialist to summon a patient.

Dr. Bard was a pudgy middle-aged man. He wore a dark blue shirt with a pale-yellow-striped tie and a white hospital uniform. His dark brown hair was combed with care and matched his light brown glasses. He resembled the typical American doctors I saw in the movies.

We shook hands. As soon as I sat down in front of him, he said bluntly, "We have reviewed your condition. You need a liver transplant."

"Transplant?" I tried to control my voice. It was a course I hadn't even thought about.

"Yes, if possible. This is the best plan, the last step we can take," he said without hesitation. "There are no other options left." Adjusting his glasses, Dr. Bard took a stack of forms from a shelf and said, "Using a goat liver or pig liver is only a medical fantasy." He paused and then continued, "You need to know, our organ supplies are scarce. There is a long waiting list. We can't guarantee at all that we can find a proper match for your liver soon."

He slid a round stool on four wheels to my side and said, "But keep your spirit up, and brace yourself with hope." He patted my shoulder. "I'll pray for you." He checked off a few items on a form and told me that most of my medical data was already available to them, but they still needed to do a few more tests before the operation. Once a suitable donor was found, they would let me know. He concluded, "You know a liver transplant is on a first-come-first-serve basis, regardless of your identity, wealth, or social status. We don't set priorities."

"I know," I said, unable to nod.

I had little recollection of how I got through those tests. I just remembered a blonde girl who led me from one room to another, from one smiling face to another. My wife called me in the middle, and I couldn't seem to answer, as I didn't know what to say. Tell her I need a new liver, but the organ supplies were scarce?

THE GALE that carried the sleet smashed across the land. Countless ice pellets rolled on the translucent ground. Sky and earth appeared to have flipped ninety degrees, and everything was shrouded in the ice. If "pouring rain" is used to describe rainstorms, I don't know how to describe this snowstorm.

The hospital waiting area was packed with people. Everyone stared out the windows in a daze. I sat down in a corner, looking through the glass at the end of the corridor and straight into the distance, feeling as heavy as the dark clouds outside.

Dr. Bard told me that my liver condition had deteriorated faster than they had expected. "I hope to switch out your liver within two months." Which implied I would die if I didn't receive a suitable donor organ in time. In other words, the doctor had sentenced me to death with a two-month suspension.

With my eyes closed, I tried to control the panic with rationality.

I recalled the morning two months ago when it had taken me twice as long as usual and a lot of exertion to arrive at work. All the scenery outside the window seemed to be floating; the music from the radio was crawling and out of tune. I tried to park my car but failed a few times. I sat in the car for another minute and wanted to try again, but I had exhausted myself.

The company's security guard knocked on my car window. "Are you all right, sir? We've been watching you." He bent down to get closer to my window. "You don't look well. Do you want to see a doctor?"

"No, thank you!" I said, shaking my head feebly.

I had urgent lab work to finish in the morning and present in the afternoon. Besides, I had to go to work. I didn't want my boss to know I was sick again. I felt that my life was like climbing a ladder. As I climbed upwards, the ladder kept rising, never-ending. However, at this moment, I felt too tired, unable to continue! I had used up all my strength to stay alive.

"Thanks!" I repeated to the security guard still standing by my window, figuring I might just need to take a break and would be all right after a while.

They sent me to the hospital after I fell into a coma. I knew from that day, my liver disease was getting worse.

This year's weather had been freaky. It was so cold in winter in the southern part of America. Last month, a torrential rainstorm that lasted twenty hours had flooded about half of the houses in the city. Everyone was still in shock.

Last week, I'd discussed the weather on the phone with my son, who was attending college on the West Coast. "Someone needs to rewrite the theory of global warming," I said.

"You're a technologist by training, but you don't seem to understand the difference between weather and climate."

"The technology I studied doesn't include God's work."

My son explained that global warming causes the temperature to rise in the Arctic, melting part of the glaciers there, stirring the stable cold air mass and pushing it straight down to reach the southernmost part of the United States.

Would global warming make a difference to me, knowing that I had just two months left to live? Who was ahead of me on the waiting list? I didn't know. There must be a lot of people. I was distraught. Life was like a meandering glacier; nobody knew where it would end till the last day. I hadn't been prepared when my life was about to collapse. Scared, I felt like my heart was squeezing out of my throat.

The wind was getting weaker. The large snowflakes fell silently down from the sky, and in a short time, they covered the trees, houses, and roads with thick snow, stranding the people in the hospital. There weren't many cars on the road, except a fearless few. The weather conditions were broadcast live on the high-hanging TV screens in the hospital lobby, with various color images rolling up and down.

I took out my phone, wanting to tell my wife I was finished here. As soon as the phone number appeared on the screen, I shut it. Damn it! I didn't know what I was doing. Could anyone get out in this weather?

A gaunt old woman came over and placed her wheeled walker beside my seat and sat down next to me, with one seat separating us. While muttering to herself, she sorted out various forms in her hands and then told me across the seat that she hadn't experienced this weather for decades. I nodded in agreement. At the moment, I craved solitude to ease my baffled mind.

Soothing music played in the hall, mixed with all the noise in the background. I felt drowsiness and an unprecedented relief. When a man puts down his assumed obligation, what else is left to worry about in life?

In the operating room, I lay still on the table. The doctors' faces dangled over my head. A surgeon with a white beard smiled and let me know they had taken out my diseased liver, yet they hadn't found a match. It would take around two months. *You lie here in peace, we'll see you in two months*. After that, the shadowless lamp over my head dimmed. As the sound of the collision of the scalpels and scissors ended, I heard the door shut gently. I shouted, "No! No! Don't leave me!" No response, only the sound of blood dripping from the lower half of my body…

IN THE DISTANCE came a faint rumbling sound, growing louder and louder. I struggled to open my eyes, and when I finally succeeded, a helicopter was nearing the top of my head. The noise was deafening, and the snowflakes kicked up from the ground flew everywhere. The sudden sight made me afraid; for a minute, I couldn't figure out what was happening. My chest felt squeezed again. When I looked at my surroundings, I realized I was still in the hospital. A medical emergency helicopter was trying to land on the snow-covered lawn next to the building.

Under the immense blades of the helicopter, they carried a man out and rolled him into the emergency center. It was all quiet again. The snow continued to fall in silence.

Time passed, little by little.

The snow didn't look like it would stop soon. In the middle, I took a call from my wife, but I didn't tell her I needed a liver transplant as I didn't want her to worry about me. Living in a foreign country for so many years, not a single step was easy.

On the other side of the waiting hall, I saw the blonde girl who had led me to the tests a few hours ago. She was walking around as though searching for someone.

Just then, a voice called over the hospital's intercom, "Mr. Chen, DaKun Chen, Dr. Bard is looking for you. Please go to Dr. Bard's office right away! DaKun Chen, Doctor Bard..." The voice sounded more urgent the second time. When I heard it for the third time, I realized they were calling me. My name is Chen DaQun, yet in the States, the family name is behind the first name. They must have misspoken the "Qun" in my first name as "Kun." I'd desired a popular American first name a long time ago, like Peter or Jack or something, but I'd felt strange making that change.

I swiftly stood up, grabbed my jacket, and met the blonde girl who was approaching. She said hurriedly, "We've been looking for you. Come with me!"

From far away, I could see Dr. Bard standing in front of his office.

"Great! I guessed you were still here." He shook my hands firmly, although we had done that a few hours before.

"Hurry and get ready for the operation," he said firmly, looking at me.

My eyes grew wide and I stared at him in disbelief. He added, "A young man didn't make it after a car accident. This damn weather!" He banged his hand on the table. "He was a voluntary organ donor. All tests showed a good match for you." His tone then turned from grief to excitement. "The snow and ice blocked all the patients in front of you, and we suspected you got stuck here too."

THIS TIME, they put me on the operating table for real.

A Blizzard

As the anesthetic seeped through my body, in front of my eyes was a white ocean connected to heaven and earth. The waves looked so soft. I ambled in and was instantly lifted up by white waves, like a baby sleeping in a cradle. I closed my eyes. The waves moved up and down gently, carrying me with them. At last, the sea began to ebb. I felt my whole body slump downwards while the snow-white water swirled around me. The sun dazzled in the white reflection. I stretched out my arms to obstruct the sun, and suddenly, both hands were caught.

"He's awake!"

I opened my eyes. A young female nurse was pressing my hands.

IV tubes were taped to the backs of my hands. An IV bottle hung on a stand next to me, and a heart rate monitor beeped a monotonous tone. At the end of the bed, My wife wearing a light-blue sterile gown, looked at me with a smile. In her face, I saw a long-lost easiness.

My eyes were wet.

The tears can share with me the pain and joy in my heart.

Over the years, traveling, working overtime, staying up late, and unbearable pressure had overloaded my body and mind. Anxiety and depression often visited me in turns. I felt sorry for myself. The disease was like a rebellious child. It was because we didn't give the body enough care that it rebelled. *If you hadn't pushed it to the brink, it might not be the way it is today.*

I would be kind to myself and to my new partner.

I wanted to meet the donor's parents, to tell them I was

sorry for their loss and that I knew how lucky I was. If they wished, I could be their son. I wanted to introduce my family to them and could do a lot for them.

THE HEAVY SNOW stopped the next day. Everything appeared so bright under the crystal-blue sky.

This extraordinary coincidence gave me a real sense of what it felt like to be alive. *It's wonderful to be alive!*

The door opened. Outside, doctors and nurses hurried by. Only then did I realize I loved it here, loved everything here!

结

从波士顿飞往伦敦的飞机开始平稳地降落。透过一层薄薄的雾气,伦敦郊区的一排排连体别墅徐徐而过。我再一次检查了携带的东西,特别是那套摄影设备,开始做好下飞机前的准备。

飞机刚停稳,爱德华的电话就打进来了:"到了吗?"

"刚到。"我正在拉头顶上的行李。

"我这就动身去机场。"他说一口英国口音。

我赶忙说:"别,千万别来。婚礼前有太多的事情要忙。别为我分心。我打个车过去就行了。"

"你就待在机场别动。"他口气匆匆,就怕我挂了电话。"再过一个小时,杰克他们乘坐的飞机就要到了。我把你们顺道一块儿接过来。"

我知道杰克和他的父母今天也要从北京过来。

宽大的伦敦候机大厅里人来人往,广播里用几种语言播放着各种航班的登机信息。既然多了一个小时,我放慢了脚步,在杰克他们下飞机的登机口附近,选了一个咖啡厅坐了下来。

爱德华是我在北京认识的朋友。在伦敦长大的他,大学毕业后在北京找了份工作。来自波士顿的我,也想在北京寻找机会。后来,我们成了室友。

杰克是个挺腼腆的山东小伙子。我和他仅仅见过一面,知道他是家里的独子,正巧和我母亲是老乡。

爱德华和杰克是在北京的一个同志俱乐部认识的。他曾带我去过一次那儿。它看起来像一个小酒吧,来的都是清一色的男性,连俱乐部里的服务生也是。烟、酒、咖啡、吉他——一切似乎都很平常。他们大部分是一对一对的,没有外人想像的那种不堪,你最多看到他们手拉着手。在这里同性恋者不是异类,他们被全盘接受。这就是他们的生活方式和权利。

这是爱德华第一次见杰克的父母。连我都有些紧张。好在在机场这种特定的环境中,似乎一切都能被冲淡。

当杰克一家从登机口出现时,我先用中文和他们打招呼。听到我这带有山东口音的中文时,他们那紧张的面容略有些松弛。

"这就是我们这次的摄影师。"爱德华向他们介绍我时,省略掉了婚礼两个字。

"我是专业里面业余的。"我连忙谦虚地说。

"应该是业余里面专业的。"爱德华纠正我,他想轻松一下气氛。我们都笑了。

在杰克他们的行李中,一只大红色的箱子格外醒目。

. . .

第二天清晨，重重的雾气还没散去。在爱德华家的后院，大家正忙着为今天的婚礼做着各种准备。

这是一幢典型的英式别墅。暖暖的红色外墙上爬满了绿色的藤状植物。宽大的后院被木栅栏围起。齐腰高的黄色连翘紧紧靠着木栅栏。一棵高大的樱桃树占据了半个后院。一阵风吹过，满树的小樱桃随风晃动。

参加这次婚礼的人数不多：双方父母，一对爱德华父母的老朋友，再就是爱德华的妹妹和他四个从小一起长大的童年伙伴。他们有个自己的小乐队。

微风拂过半开的窗户，带着淡淡的烤面包的香味。爱德华的母亲正在厨房里忙碌着，此刻，她正为已经完成的婚礼蛋糕做最后的装点。为了能亲手给儿子做婚礼蛋糕，她还专门去上了烘培培训班。我在厨房帮着她打下手。两年前，我来伦敦旅行时在这儿小住过几天，已经和他们很熟了。这次来就随意多了。

爱德华的父母都已从剑桥大学退休，父亲曾是哲学系教授，母亲教的是历史。家里书房四周沿墙的书架上摆满了各种书籍。大多数时间他们在这里读书、写作、讨论世界上发生的各种事情，为此常常争论得很激烈。他们也非常喜欢中国文化。这是一对和蔼的老人，幽默、睿智、博学。和他们聊天是一种享受。

厨房里我们一边忙着一边聊着。他们想做一道地道的中国菜，我贡献了鲁式红烧肉。——这是我在家向妈妈学的最拿手的菜。几天前，他们就备好了所有必要的食材。这会儿，肉香已经弥漫在厨房的各个角落。

在聊天中我们聊的最多是爱德华，还有他这桩特殊的婚姻。记得在北京三里屯的那套二居室里，爱德华就为怎样向父母解释这段恋情而担心过。虽然在西方长大的孩子会比中国孩子在婚姻恋爱上有更多的自由，他还是担心已经年迈的父母是否能坦然接受。

记得一天早晨，爱德华敲着我的房门，兴奋地说："杨，我妈刚回的邮件。他们同意了。我太高兴了！真的感谢他们的理解。"

我曾经从头到尾读过他母亲的那份邮件。至今，我还清楚地记得这么几段话：上天给了我们各种生活方式。既然我们选定了其中的一种，那么就走下去。逃离不是一个正确的态度，因为你逃离的不是你的生活，而是你自己。

对待生命你不妨大胆冒险一点，因为，好歹你要失去它。

最后这一句，爱德华妈妈引用了尼采的话。

我真为爱德华高兴。

透过厨房大玻璃窗正好能看到后院，婚礼的准备似乎也已就绪。

爱德华父亲一边拍着身上的尘土，一边笑呵呵地走进来说："莫琳，我可以向你保证一切都准备好了。"说完他向我们做了一个OK的手势，又朝我诙谐地挤了一下左眼。随后他又吸了吸鼻子说："这里烧的什么好东西？太香了！把我肚子里的馋虫都钩出来了。"

"这是扬做的拿手好菜。——鲁式红烧肉。希望杰克的父母喜欢。"爱德华母亲说完，用左臂碰了我一下。

突然，她放下手中的碟子，边解围裙边喊着："哈罗德，抓紧时间。我们该去梳妆打扮了。我可不想让杰克的父母看到我现在这个样子。"临走时还朝我做了个鬼脸。

院子里，爱德华正陪着他的四个伙伴聊天。他向我一一介绍了每一位，还特意拉过来有着一头黄色卷发、高个儿的里奇，得意地对我说："这就是我以前常向你提起的那个著名的吉他手。"

我羡慕地向他点点头说："爱德华经常提起你。见到你很荣幸。"

"听到他的演奏你将会更荣幸。"说完爱德华搂着我的肩笑起来。里奇也羞涩地笑了笑，耸了耸肩膀。

阳光渗过层层的枝叶，斑驳陆离地洒在院子的地上。修剪整齐的绿色草坪上，小乐队已经摆好了各自的位置。

爱德华的父母已经梳妆整齐。让我吃惊的是，老太太穿了一件中式高领绸缎上衣。淡灰色的底料上斜绣着一只绿色的孔雀，配上她的蓝眼睛和高鼻梁，颇有一种特别的风味。大家欢呼起来，乐手们把乐器敲得叮当响。她把双手斜握在右侧，膝盖微微向下一弯，行了一个古代宫庭礼。大家一阵哄笑。里奇还把两个手指放进嘴里打了一个长长的口哨。

也许是时差或别的什么原因，尽管杰克一家住的酒店离这儿并不太远，他们比预定的时间还是迟来了一会儿。

我站在爱德华一家人的身后，看着他们热情地欢迎杰克一家人。最后，杰克把那只大红色的行李箱拉了进来。这箱子和他妈穿的那件红色的短呢子大衣一样醒目。

杰克忙着翻译两边的对话，额头上微微地冒出了一些细汗。我连忙靠近他说："这边的事情交给我吧。你去准备准备。"

他感激地朝我点点头。从他的表情可以看出,他似乎在控制不断积累着的不安情绪。

我这次来,除了摄影还要兼做翻译。我的中文不错,这要归功于来美国三十年的妈妈。她要求我必须在家里百分之百说中文。记得有一段时间,我实在烦于在两种语言里蹦来蹦去,就采取了一种折中的办法。她说中文,我用英语回答。没想到刚开始我就败下阵来,她装着听不懂,根本不与理睬。

在一个角落里,杰克妈妈悄悄地问我结婚了没有。我告诉她刚谈了一个女朋友。听到这句话,她看我的眼光瞬间暗淡下来。随后,她又用手指了指杰克用更低的声音说:"他是咋回事?我们都弄不明白。"

我张了张嘴想说点什么,又把话吞了回去。说实话,这个问题太复杂了,它牵涉到生理学、心理学和社会学,可能还有些不为人知的什么学。这些都需要专家们来解释。也许是天生的,也许是后天的。我无能为力。仅仅得到一个解释,他们就能释怀吗?

我不知道该用什么表情才能让她知道我的为难。我点了点头,又摇了摇头。

院子栅栏边矮矮的醋栗伸出了枝头,上面挂满了一串串红色的小果子,像一只只小灯笼在风中摇摆,让小院增添了一些喜庆的气氛。

由于没有邀请很多宾客,当然还有一些特殊的原因,婚礼将不按照英国传统的形式举行。

院子中心摆放着两张圆桌,上面铺着雪白的桌布。每张桌上都放着插满鲜花的花瓶,还有各种英式点心、饮料和酒品,给人随意而温馨的感觉。

我把相机对准他们,努力地去捕捉珍贵的镜头。

两家父母、长辈们和一对新人坐在左边的桌上，右边的那一张留给我们这些年轻人。这一点看起来有点像中国人的规矩。

爱德华穿着一身黑色的西装，淡蓝色的衬衫上扎了一条深蓝色的紫色斜纹领带。杰克的西装是天蓝色的，雪白的衬衫上系了一个深红色的领结。这些让我大概猜出他们之间的角色。

透过镜头，我看见两位母亲坐在一起正通过杰克说着什么。杰克妈妈只是默默地点头，而大部分时间都在直楞楞地盯着儿子。有一次她想打哈欠，刚一张嘴又憋了回去。随后她拿起桌上的杯子，没喝放了下来，又呆滞地盯着杯子。她似乎想弄明白到底发生了什么。穿在她身上的那件大红毛衣和披在肩膀上的粉红头巾，也没能掩去她略显苍白的脸色。

中间，爱德华父亲举起酒杯，向二位新婚的年青人祝福，并向杰克父母致谢，谢谢他们给爱德华带来了这么好的爱人，说他们全家都喜欢杰克，祝他们永远幸福！

这时，里奇在自己弹奏的吉他和弦中，轻轻地唱起了俄国弗拉基米尔的《燕子》。

温和的修士，我们滑翔
飞过你的修道院
飞过闪烁的湖面
泛着青绿和银光
明天，好人儿，我们将离去
……
尽管你不懂鸟鸣
啁啾犹如银铃

你仍然会抬头仰望我们
翱翔在绿松石色的穹顶

歌声很轻柔,像来自遥远。

音乐一停,杰克父亲拿出那只红箱子说:"这是我们从老家带来的新婚礼物。杰克奶奶让我们一定要在婚礼上转交给他们。这是我们那儿的风俗。"语气中显得有些无奈。

我早就注意到这个大红色的箱子了,于是迅速推进了一个特写镜头。

此刻,打开的箱子里呈现出一片红色,在阳光的照射下非常晃眼:一床龙凤呈祥的大红缎子被面;一对桃红色的鸳鸯戏水绣花枕套;一个装有红枣、花生、桂圆和栗子的红色布袋子;还有几包印有红双喜的喜糖。

爱德华母亲用双手捂住嘴巴,感叹道:"太漂亮了!太漂亮了!"

杰克向大家介绍了每一样东西。最后,当他指着那只红袋子时,声音突然停住了。我也开始紧张起来。三年前,我和妈妈回山东老家参加表姐的婚礼时,这些场面我都见过。

突然的安静,让气氛有些尴尬。

爱德华父亲颇有把握地说:"我猜,这些东西一定有特别的意义,而且很好吃。"显然,他并不知道中国传统的婚嫁风俗。

"早生贵子!"这突如其来的声音,像锤子一样砸了下来。这声音又如此凄凉。

杰克没有翻译。我,更不敢。

静;那种会把人赶跑的寂静。

杰克父亲瞥了一眼他的妻子,刚要说什么,又捂住了那句就要出口的话。他伸出手使劲地拍着儿子的肩膀，似乎想从他身上拍出一句合适的话来。接着，又用另一只手把脸抹了抹。嘴唇上露出了哆哆嗦嗦的笑容。

我从来没有遇见过这种场面，也不知道怎么来调和。

这时，杰克的母亲又用一种悲怆的声调念叨了一句："他不仅挖掉了我们的根，还把坑填得严严实实。"沙哑的声音夹着颤抖，虽然声音并不大。

我知道他们的心情，但没想到她扔出了这么苍凉的一句。我的心直直地往下沉。

镜头里，我看见她抬起头，睁大眼睛，试着忍住眼泪，然后再一次忍住。

对未来的惧怕比确切的现实更恐惧。仿佛是一种痛来自遥远。

小院里只剩下风声。

爱德华父母没有听懂这些话；但从杰克母亲说话的表情和语气中显然猜到了什么。

他们也许事先有些担心，但是他们万万没有想到，杰克父母会带着这样的心态来参加儿子的婚礼。

在中国文化中，传宗接代是天大的事情。他们对同性婚姻的容忍度有多少？能来参加儿子的婚礼已经很了不起了。

突然，爱德华母亲想起了什么。她连连喊道："红烧肉，红烧肉。"

对，我差一点忘了我的红烧肉。——那碗来自家乡的红烧肉。

如果这碗红烧肉能让他们有一丝慰藉。

. . .

中间，我的妈妈打来电话，关心婚礼进行得如何。当我说到"早生贵子"时，电话那边安静下来。一种死死的沉寂，然后是一声深深的叹息。一种做为母亲，特别是中国母亲的那种叹息。

此时，我很想告诉杰克的父母：一件事情对你的伤害与事情本身无关，而是取决于你对这件事情的态度。我还想告诉他们：上天会眷顾你们的儿子。无法改变的事要默默承受。后来我什么都没说，说什么都是苍白的。

吉他又响了，声音宛如来自遥远。

> ……
> *尽管你不懂得鸟鸣*
> *啁啾犹如银铃*
> *你仍然会抬头仰望我们*
> *翱翔在绿松石色的穹顶*

THE KNOT

∽

The plane from Boston to London began its smooth descent. Through a thin layer of mist, the rows of townhouses in the suburbs of London crept past. Once again, I checked my carry-on, especially the camera gear, before arrival.

Edward's call came in when the plane had just stopped. "Got here?"

"Just arrived," I said, pulling the luggage out of the overhead bins.

"I'm leaving for the airport," he said with a heavy British accent.

"Don't. Don't come," I said hastily. "There are so many things to do before the wedding. Don't get diverted by me. I'll just take a cab."

"You stay at the airport, don't move," he said hurriedly,

afraid that I would hang up. "Jack's plane is arriving in an hour. I'll take you along."

I knew Jack and his parents were coming from Beijing today.

The extensive London airport terminal was bustling with people, the loudspeakers broadcasting the boarding information for various flights in several languages. Now with an extra hour to spare, I decided to relax and chose a café near Jack's gate to sit down in.

Edward was a friend I'd met in China. He'd grown up in London and found a job in Beijing after college. I was from Boston and had also wanted to look for opportunities in Beijing. Later, we'd become roommates.

Jack was a timid young man from Shandong province. He and I had only met once, and I knew he was the only child in his family. Coincidentally, he was from the same town where my mother had grown up.

Edward and Jack had met at a gay club in Beijing. Edward had taken me there once. It resembled a small bar, but all the people there were guys, including the servers. It seemed just like any other club, with drinks and live music—nothing looked out of the ordinary. Most of them were in pairs, not as bad as outsiders would imagine. At most you'd see men holding hands. Here gay men are not unusual, and they're all accepted. It's their way of life, their rights.

This was Edward's first time meeting Jack's parents. Even I was a bit nervous. Luckily, the surroundings in the airport terminal seemed to dilute everything.

As Jack's family emerged from the gate, I greeted them

in Chinese. Their tight faces relaxed slightly when they heard my Shandong accent.

"This is our photographer," Edward introduced me, omitting the word *wedding*.

"I'm a professional amateur," I said humbly.

"You should be an amateur professional," Edward corrected, trying to lighten the mood. We all laughed.

When we picked up their luggage, a bright red suitcase was eye-catching.

THE NEXT MORNING, people had started preparing for today's wedding in the backyard of Edward's house before the heavy fog had dispersed.

It was a classic English-style villa. Green vines covered the warm red-tone exterior wall. A wooden fence enclosed the large backyard. The waist-high yellow forsythia clung to the fence. A tall cherry tree shadowed half the backyard. Many little cherries were jiggling in the breeze.

The guest list was small: both sets of parents, an old friend of Edward's parents, Edward's sister and four childhood friends who had all grown up together. They had a small band of their own.

The breeze blew through the half-opened window, carrying the aroma of freshly baked bread. Edward's mother was busy in the kitchen, putting the final touches on the wedding cake. To make this cake personally for her son, she'd attended a baking class. I was helping her in the kitchen. When visiting London two years ago, I'd stayed here for a few days and become acquainted with them. It was a lot more casual this time.

Edward's parents had retired from Cambridge University, where the father had been a professor of philosophy and the mother had taught history. The bookshelves along the walls of their study were full of books. They spend most of their time here reading, writing, and discussing current world affairs, which often led to fierce debates. They were also fond of Chinese culture. They were a sweet old couple, humorous, wise, and knowledgeable. Conversing with them was a real treat.

We were chatting while busy in the kitchen. They wanted to make an authentic Chinese dish. I contributed a Shandong-style braised pork—the best dish I had learned from my mother at home. They had prepared all the ingredients for me a few days ago. At this moment, the scent of the meat had permeated every corner of the kitchen.

During the conversation, we talked mostly about Edward and his special marriage. I recollected how, in the two-bedroom apartment in Sanlitun, Beijing, Edward had been stressed over how to explain his relationship with Jack to his parents. While youngsters in the West had more freedom than their Chinese counterparts when it came to love and marriage, he still worried about whether his elderly parents would accept them.

One morning, Edward knocked on my door and exclaimed, "Yang, my mother replied to my email. They agreed. I'm so happy that they understand!"

I read his mother's email from beginning to end. To

this day, I could still remember a few paragraphs: God gave us many ways of life. Now that we have chosen one, let's move on. Escape is not a correct state of mind because you're not fleeing from your life but rather yourself.

When managing your life, you may as well take a chance, for you'll lose it, regardless of how it will be.

In the last sentence, Edward's mother quoted Nietzsche.

I was excited for Edward.

THROUGH THE LARGE window in the kitchen, I saw the preparations for the wedding in the backyard seemed complete.

"Maureen, I can assure you everything is ready," Edward's father came in and said, grinning as he brushed off some dust from his side. With that, he made an OK gesture to us and squeezed his left eye. Then he sniffed and said, "What's the good stuff cooking here? It smells great, giving me a big appetite!"

"It's a specialty dish made by Yang, Shandong-style braised pork. I hope Jack's parents like it," said Edward's mother, nudging me with her left arm.

Abruptly, she put down her saucer and shouted, "Harold, hurry. We need to get dressed. I don't want Jack's parents to see me like this." She grimaced at me when she cleared out.

In the backyard, Edward was chatting with his four friends. He introduced each of them to me and specially pulled over a tall guy, Rich, with curly yellow hair. "This is the famous guitarist I often mentioned to you," he boasted.

I nodded admiringly and said, "Edward often speaks of you. It is a pleasure to meet you."

"You'll be more honored to hear him play." Edward put his arm around my shoulder and grinned. Rich chuckled and shrugged his shoulders.

The sunlight filtered through the layers of leaves and scattered over the garden ground. The members of the small band had taken their respective positions on the manicured green lawn.

Edward's parents were neatly dressed. To my surprise, his mother wore a Chinese-style high-collared silk blouse with a green peacock embroidered on the light gray base, which set off her blue eyes and high nose, revealing a unique taste. Everyone cheered, and the musicians clanked their instruments. She held her hands to the right, with her knees down, and performed an ancient palace greeting. We all burst into laughter. Rich put two fingers in his mouth and made a long whistle.

Perhaps due to jet lag or some other reason, Jack's family arrived later than planned, despite the hotel being close.

I stood behind the Edward family and watched as they warmly greeted Jack and his family. At last, Jack rolled in the bright red suitcase, as striking as his mother's short red woolen coat.

Jack was busy translating the conversations, and a little

sweat appeared on his forehead. I hurried to him and said, "Let me take care of this. You go get ready."

He nodded gratefully. Judging from his expression, he was trying to control a growing uneasiness.

Besides being a photographer, I was also an interpreter at the time. I spoke good Chinese, thanks to my mom, who had come to America thirty years earlier. She'd asked me to speak one hundred percent Chinese at home. There was a period when I had been tired of switching between two languages and struck a compromise. She spoke Chinese to me, and I answered in English. Yet I fizzled from the beginning, since she ignored me by pretending not to understand me.

In a corner, Jack's mother quietly asked me, "Are you married?" I told her I only had a girlfriend. When she heard this, her eyes dimmed right away. Then she pointed to Jack and lowered her voice. "What's the matter with him? We don't get it."

I opened my mouth, wanting to say something, but I gulped it back. To be honest, this subject must be so complicated, involving physiology, psychology, sociology, and perhaps some obscure science. Maybe it was natural, or maybe it was acquired later in life. It required an expert to explain. There was nothing I could help with. Would they feel relieved simply to hear an explanation?

I didn't know what expression I should use to make her aware of my dilemma. I nodded and then shook my head.

The dwarf gooseberry at the edge of the yard stretched out its branches hung with strings of little red fruits, like small lanterns swinging in the breeze, adding to the festive atmosphere.

Since there were only a few guests, and because of the particular circumstances surrounding the wedding, it wasn't set up to follow the British tradition.

There were two round tables covered with snow-white tablecloths in the center of the backyard, each stocked with vases full of flowers, an assortment of English snacks, wines and other beverages, creating a sense of ease and warmth.

I positioned my camera, trying to capture some precious shots.

The parents, elders and the newlyweds sat at the table to the left, leaving the one on the right for young people, which seemed to conform the Chinese custom.

Edward wore a black suit and a light blue shirt with a dark-blue twill tie. Jack's suit was sky blue, and he wore a white shirt and a crimson bow tie, offering me a hint at the roles between them.

Through the lens, I saw the two mothers sitting together, talking about something through Jack. His mother nodded quietly, and most of the time she gazed directly at her son. Once, she wanted to yawn but struggled to hold back. She grabbed the glass from the table yet put it back down again with a dull look in her eyes. A second later, she stared at her son again, as if trying to make sense of what had transpired. The bright red sweater she wore and the pink scarf on her shoulder couldn't hide her pale face.

In the middle, Edward's father raised his glass and blessed the two newlywed young men, thanking Jack's parents for bringing such a wonderful person into Edward's life and saying their whole family liked Jack. "May they be happy forever!"

At that moment, Rich chanted "The Swallow" by Russia's Vladimir Nabokov over his guitar chords.

> *Gentle monk, we glide*
> *above your monastery*
> *and above the lake shining*
> *bluish and silver.*
> *Tomorrow, dear sir, we will fly away*
> *......*
> *and, not understanding the birds'*
> *little ringing words*
> *you will see us above the tops*
> *of the turquoise domes*

The song was soft, as if from far away.

When the music ceased, Jack's father hauled out the red suitcase and said, "These are the wedding gifts we brought from home. Jack's grandma asked us to give them to you at the wedding. It is a custom of ours." His voice sounded hesitant.

I had long noticed this red suitcase, so I zoomed in quickly for a close-up shot.

At this moment, the suitcase was opened. Everything inside was in a bright red color, dazzling in the sunlight.

There was a scarlet comforter cover imprinted with a dragon and a phoenix; two peach-red pillowcases, each embroidered with a pair of mandarin ducks playing in the water; a red cloth sack containing red dates, peanuts, longans, and chestnuts; and a few packets of "double happiness" festive candies.

Edward's mother covered her mouth with her hands and exclaimed, "How beautiful! It's so lovely!"

Jack explained each item. At last, as he pointed at the red sack, his voice abruptly stopped. I got nervous, having seen a similar scene three years ago, when my mother and I had gone back to our hometown in Shandong to attend my cousin's wedding.

The sudden quietness made the atmosphere a little awkward.

Edward's father said with certainty, "I guess these must be something special and delicious." Obviously, he wasn't familiar with traditional Chinese marriage customs.

"*Zao Sheng Gui Zi!*" A Chinese diction of the dates, peanuts, longans, and chestnuts that, when pronounced together, meant "Have a lovely baby soon!" The voice came out of the blue like a hammer. It was so bleak.

Jack didn't translate, nor did I dare to.

Silence; the kind that would drive people away.

Jack's father glanced at his wife and wanted to say something but kept it down. He stretched out his hand and patted his son's shoulder heavily, as if he could make him say a few appropriate words. Then he wiped his face with his other hand. A shaking grin left his lips.

I had never encountered such a situation and didn't know how to defuse it.

In a sorrowful tone, Jack's mother murmured, "Not only did he dig out our roots, but he also filled the pits." Her hoarse voice trembled, though not loud.

I knew what they were feeling, but I hadn't expected she'd toss out such desolate words. My heart sank straight down.

In the viewfinder, I saw her raising her head and widening her eyes to hold back the tears, and then fighting the tears once more.

Fear of the future is more frightening than today's reality. It was as if the pain came from far away.

Only the sound of breeze remained in the backyard.

Edward's parents didn't understand those words; however, they had most likely guessed their meaning from her expression and voice.

They might have had some worries beforehand, but they'd never thought Jack's parents would come to their son's wedding with such an attitude.

In Chinese culture, it's a big deal to carry on one's family line. How much tolerance did the general public have for same-sex marriage? The fact that they'd attended their son's wedding was remarkable in itself.

Suddenly, Edward's mother remembered something. She cried out, "Braised pork, braised pork."

Yeah, I'd almost forgotten my braised pork—the dish from my hometown.

If only it could give them a trace of comfort.

In the middle of all this, my mom called and asked

about how the wedding was going. When I mentioned "*Zao Sheng Gui Zi!*" there was a dead silence, followed by a deep sigh. The sigh of a mother, especially a Chinese mother.

I wanted to tell Jack's parents that the harm a matter does to you isn't in itself, but in your disposition towards it. I also wanted to say, "God will take care of your son. What cannot be changed shall be endured in silence." But I said nothing, as that would have sounded so weak.

The guitar played again, and the music seemed to come from far away.

> ......
>
> *and, not understanding the birds'*
> *little ringing words*
> *you will see us above the tops*
> *of the turquoise domes*

国家福利

公交车刚停稳门就开了。老头用劲地把老伴推上车后,前脚刚踏上第一个台阶,老伴就转身嚷嚷着要下来。

"怎么了?"老头说。

"赶紧下!赶紧下!"老伴说着,踉踉跄跄地从公交车的台阶上哧溜下来。

老头一把扶稳她说:"怎么了?好不容易才等来一辆车,这会儿都已经迟了。你还去不去啊?"老头一急,满脸的皱纹挤到了一起。

老伴拍了拍衣服口袋,有些歉意地说:"嘿,刚才换衣服时把交通卡落下了。"

"我以为什么事呢,不就是两块钱吗?"老头说,"已经都等了这么久了,再算上从家走到车站的时间,你穷折腾什么?"

一般过了上班高峰，公交车通勤时间就拉长了。平均要花二十分钟才能等来一辆。

老伴瞥了老头一眼："怎么是两块钱？来回可不就是四块钱了。"接着她凑近老头把声音压低说："你看，我们原本是去吃免费餐的，这样搭上四块钱，跑这一趟还有啥意思？"

老头听老伴这么一说，感觉有道理。脸上的皱纹也就舒展开了。他嘟囔了一句："是的，现在最不值钱的就是时间了。"

当他们再次登上公交车时，已经又过去半个小时了。

"早晨好！"司机托尼热情地和他们打招呼。

等他们坐稳后，托尼又说："今天的天气真好！你们还是去教堂吗？"

看样子他们是老乘客了。

"是的，是的。"老头一边点头一边微笑，用带有口音的英语回答。

虽然老夫妻俩已经来美国七、八年了，可是他们的英语还在"是和不是，好和不好"的水平上打转转。女儿一直催着他们多花点时间学好英语，他们却一直推脱年纪太大了，记性跟不上。每次托尼见到他们总想多聊几句，可是没说上两句就没下文了。有时他们连点头摇头都不在点子上。好在他们能把上下车的站牌牢牢地记住，从来没有出过任何差错。

他们要去的教堂是美国西部最普通的一种教堂。如果不是屋顶上的十字架和几块镶嵌着圣母马丽亚的彩色玻璃窗，你一定以为这里是个大仓库。和欧洲那些动则需要建造几百年，且气势恢弘、异彩纷呈，并有着高耸入云的尖顶的雄伟大教堂相比，真让人怀疑这些美国人对上帝到底有几分的虔诚。好在他们有着各种乐善好施的行为，也许上帝可以原谅他们。这里每个星期两次向穷人开放的免费午餐，就是其中之一。

等到老俩口气喘吁吁地赶到教堂侧面的餐厅时，免费午餐已经开始有一会儿了。一排排长条桌边挤挤挨挨坐满了人。各种混杂的气味在大厅里弥漫着。

大门左边的长桌上，放着几盆热气腾腾的食物。几个热情的自愿者们正在忙碌着。看到他们进来，一头红色卷发的玛丽微笑着说："今天你们来得晚了点。"

"是的，是的。"老头连忙点头，拿起盘子去接玛丽送来的食物。

旁边的老伴捅了捅他小声说："别要那么多土豆和面包，不值钱。"

"好的，好的。"老头一边往前挪着，一边扭过头朝远处的人堆里张望。他想看看王珊老太太来了没有。

"给我来两份牛肉圆子。"老伴用中文说了一句。——其实她是说给老头听的。然后，她向玛丽旁边的小伙子竖起食指和中指，又指了指盆里的牛肉圆子。

两份真的不少。老头有点不好意思往老伴的盘子里看。

每次来吃免费午餐的基本上是两类人：一类是穿着油腻腻的衣服，身上散发着一股酸味的无家可归的流浪汉。一般他们挑一个角落坐下来默默地吃着。另一类是上了年纪的中国大爷大妈。他们大声地吃着、说着、笑着。

餐厅里另一边，王珊老太太看到了正在门口取食物的老头。她站起身来向这边用力挥手。脖子上的大红围巾格外显眼。

老头刚要挪动脚步往那边走。老伴一把抓住他，用嘴努了努附近的两个座位，然后仰起脸朝王珊老太太大声地喊："今天我们就坐这里了，您慢慢吃。"

老头有些闷闷不乐。老伴没好气地问："每次你来这里，是不是就想来见她？"

"你说什么呢？都这么一把年纪了，不就是谈得来吗？"

"这么多人，你只和她谈得来？"一丝不快渗入话里。

老头把头转向一边，懒得理她。

第二天一大早，住在同一层老年公寓的老张打来电话，告诉他们今天九华超市有很多东西打五折，问要不要一起去。老俩口正在吃早饭。老伴连声说："好，好。我们这就过去。"其实昨天从教堂带回来的食物还足够他们再吃一阵子。

"你就不怕我又踫见王珊？"老头昨天的气还没全消。

"你们还真有什么事？"她的音量陡升。

老头不说话了。每到这个时候，他总是首先退出。

超市里人头攒动。各种打折的商品上贴着红红绿绿的标签。老年公寓的老头老太们都出动了。

新鲜玉米大降价——打三折！堆着玉米的大篓子边上挤满了老头老太。四周到处丢的都是玉米外衣；剥开又不要的玉米随手又被扔回篓子里。超市的工作人员跑前跑后地忙着清理。

老头的手机响了。是女儿打过来的。女儿说，妈怎么样了？你昨晚说她心脏不舒服，需要我请假带她去看医生吗？老头说，不用，这次没事。昨天她吃了太多的牛肉圆子。女儿说，那就好好休息。我这几天公司很忙。老头又说，我和你妈正在超市买东西。今天很多东西都打折。我们已经买了很多。女儿说，让我怎么说你们？老命都不要了。真是疯了！女儿的声音中夹着控制不住的怒气。

当老俩口推着满满一小车食品回到家时，老梁教授已经站在门口等了他们有一会了。这位梁教授是他们的钟点工，每天上午十点准时到达。政府为这个年龄层的穷人都配了钟点工。

老梁是国内沿海地区一所大学的教授。他看上去六十多，中等个儿，略有些秃顶。如果没有人说，还真看不出他曾经是大学教授。

"两位老领导又去买菜啦。"老梁满脸堆着笑，嗓门洪亮。

在国内，老头和老伴曾经是领导，大概一个是副厅级，一个是正处级。老梁第一次到这里来做工时就这么称呼他们。一是他们年长他十几岁；二是他们的的确确当过领导；再就是嘴甜总没有坏处。

门开了。这是一个典型的小户型老人公寓，一间客厅，一间卧室，外加厨房和浴室。里里外外被老梁收拾得干干净净。

老梁接过大包小包的食品，一件件往冰箱里塞。

他有些发愁地说："老领导，不能再买了。冰箱已经太满了。昨天拿回来的两袋面包只能放在外面了。"

"行，行。你看着办吧。一切都交给你了。"老头说。

自从老梁来了这半年，老头轻松了许多。虽然老梁在国内没做过多少家务活，但通过这几年的锻炼很有长进。他烧的一手南方菜,让老俩口赞不绝口。当然,这十几美元一小时的工钱让老梁赚得很开心。轻轻松松,边聊边做,一上午三十多美元就到手了。所以,他做事很上心。

厨房里,老梁开始做午饭了。

老俩口打开电视,在茶几两边的沙发椅上坐了下来。老头一般不和老伴争,她想看什么频道,他就跟着看。最近,老伴迷上了国内的财经节目。屏目上红红绿绿的数字常让她异常兴奋。

"老梁,你买股票吗?"她对着厨房大声问道。

"不敢,不敢。"老梁从厨房伸出头来答道,"我们这个年纪手上这点钱都是保命钱。"

"我是说用国内的退休金买。"老伴说。

老梁一步从厨房跨了出来,把食指竖在嘴上,示意她小点声。老伴捂住了嘴巴。

老梁拿了一把韭菜坐了下来。一边挑拣着一边和他们聊起来:"美国国家福利让我们衣食不愁啊!"

老伴跟着感慨道:"是啊!老了就怕生病。这里看病不用花钱,真是百病无忧呀!"她有些笑得合不拢嘴,接着又说:"再加上每月一千多美元的补助,真是花都花不完。"

大家都笑了。

老伴又说:"子女是靠不住的。真的没想到老了老了还攀上个'亲娘'。"

老头有点不同意了,瞥了一眼老伴说:"没有女儿帮我们办移民,我们能过来吗?"

"那当然不行。"老伴不否定。

"如果这么算的话,"老梁说,"你们那些在国内存的退休金还真的可以考虑买一些股票。"不过他又立即补充了一句,"这事你们自己决定,别听我的。"说完,他拿起摘好的韭菜回厨房了。

没过一会儿,几盘香味扑鼻的菜就端上了桌子。老梁又用余下的时间清洁了房子。最后他收拾垃圾,结束了今天的活儿。

"老梁,要不要留下来一起吃午饭?家里东西多。"老头热情地挽留他。

"不用,不用。"老梁说,"等一会儿还要去楼上的陈老板家干活。"

老梁说的那个陈老板,来美国前经营了一家公司。所以大家也跟着称呼他老板。

"听说昨天为了什么事,陈老板的儿子过来和他们俩口子大吵了一架。"老伴插话进来。

"听说了,吵得挺凶。儿子放出狠话,说是不认他们了。"老梁说,"好像是关于打911的事。"

老伴突然想起什么,说:"怪不得昨天看见救护车过来了。"

老梁凑近他们小声说:"其实陈老板并没有什么大病,只是血压有些高。他不想打扰儿子,又不想花钱打车,直接就打911了。这样又快、又省钱、又省事。"

老头说:"老年人打车有优惠。不就几块钱吗?"

"是啊。"老梁说,"要不说儿子气得不认他们了呢。昨天救护车一到,医院马上就通知了他的儿子。儿子觉得他们这事做得特别过分。"

老头忧心忡忡地说:"这样的事再来几次,下次真的遇到危急情况,也没人来救咱们了。"

几天的财经节目看下来,老伴越来越有信心了。

国内的股市连着几天都是直线上涨，不少股票都出现了涨停板。老伴真的有些坐不住了。她后悔没有早点下手。

前几天，儿子从国内打来电话，说他们存在银行里的几十万人民币退休金到期了，问是否要再继续存一样的定期。老伴告诉儿子，这笔钱暂时用不上，不如买股票。

昨天儿子又来电话说，全部钱都买了股票基金。也就是说，从现在开始，她就是真枪实弹地干了。屏目上出现的红红绿绿的数字确确实实和她有着不可分割的联系了。

老头一再提醒老伴，这把年纪玩股票是不是太离谱，但她总是指着屏幕上交易厅里的一群老头老太说，就是这把年纪才有时间玩股票，而且动脑筋能防老年呆痴。老头说不过她。

一个星期过去了，又是一个星期的连连涨。老伴志得意满、喜不自禁。这几天她天天拉着老梁，向他描述股票上涨的盛况，弄得老梁多多少少都有些心生悔意。不过老梁还是一再提醒她：股市有风险！

老头也拿老伴没办法。只要她高兴就好。

连续的涨势，在星期一戛然而止，停止得那么突然。这么多天都是红色的数字，蓦然间，锋回路转，一派愁云惨淡。星期二是这样，星期三还是这样。老头换了频道，不让老伴再盯着看了。

"你还要不要命了？你不是总说我们不缺钱吗？这避之唯恐不及的中国股市，你也敢往里跳？在咱们这把年龄，你……"老头看老伴不说话了，觉得自己有些急不择言，就把后面的话咽了回去，又反过来安慰她，"我们有美国的国家福利，那些钱丢了也就丢了吧。"

在这个家里，老伴的心情是头等大事。

很少收到信件的老年公寓，这几天家家都收到了一封信。信，是从美国社会安全局寄来的。

老俩口完全看不懂。他们打电话让女儿过来一趟。女儿说，这几天特别忙，周末一定过来。她提醒他们，可以先让老梁帮着看看。在这幢楼里没有人的英文比老梁的好了。

上午十点，老梁一进门就提到了这封信。他说自己也收到了一封。

老头连忙拿出这封信，让老梁逐字逐句地解释给他们听。老梁戴上老花镜坐了下来。看得出，他的心情颇有些沉重。

信的内容大致是这样的：现在要重新开始申请美国国家福利。每户要在一个月内提交在美国所有银行的户头信息，并报告在他国领取退休金的金额。否则，将取消在美国领取福利的资格。

老伴心里一惊，不过很快就平静下来了。她很清楚，她和老头在美国银行只有一个户头，里面就存了几百美元。另外几万美元现金一直都锁在家里的箱子里。其实这里的老人们都知道，如果在美国银行的存款超过两千美元，就领不到国家福利了。

"老梁，请你说得再慢一点。刚才提到的退休金是怎么回事？"老伴打断了老梁的话。她的声音有些惊惶。

老梁把刚才读过的那些话又重复了一遍。

"那要是不报在中国的养老收入呢？"老头想竭力控制住自己的声调。老头知道，他和老伴在国内每个月大约一千七百美元的养老收入从来没有申报过。很多这里拿福利的中国老人也从来都没有申报过。他们很清楚，如果让美国政府知道他们在中国还有另外一份养老收入的话，他们在美国的国家福利将被彻底取消。

"如果你刻意隐瞒在他国的养老收入，"——老梁的声音开始颤抖起来——"靠欺诈的办法从联邦政府获得福利，将被判以六个月的监禁。这个判决不得上诉。同时吊销你在美国的移民身份。"

刺耳的警笛声由远至近，救护车很快就停在老年公寓的门口。车顶上红蓝色的灯光，一闪一闪交替地打在大楼的墙壁上。

老头神情茫然地坐在不省人事的老伴身边，混浊的眼泪顺着满是皱纹的脸颊，弯弯曲曲地流下来。

他嚅动着双唇喃喃道："国家福利，国家福利……"

NATIONAL WELFARE

~

Hardly had the bus stopped when the door opened. The old man pushed his wife into the bus with all his strength. As he set his foot on the first step, the old lady turned around and shouted at him to get down.

"What's the matter?" he asked.

"Hurry, get down, get down," the wife said as she stumbled over the steps.

The old man steadied her. "What? Getting a bus was difficult. We're already late. Are you still going?" The old man's face creased in a rush.

The wife patted her pocket and said apologetically, "Hey, I left the transportation card behind when I was changing."

"What's the big deal? It's only two dollars. We've been

waiting so long, and if you count the time from home to the station…"

The buses didn't run as often after the rush hour. It took an average of twenty minutes to get one.

The wife glanced at the old man. "Why only two dollars? It's four dollars back and forth." Then she leaned close to the old man and lowered her voice. "We go there for a free lunch. What's the point of spending four dollars to get there and back?"

The old man saw the logic in this. The wrinkles on his face smoothed. "Yes, the least valuable thing now is time," he mumbled.

It was half an hour later when they stepped on the bus again.

"Good morning!" Driver Tony greeted them warmly. Seeing them settled down, Tony said, "It's a lovely day! Are you still going to the church?"

It looked like they were regular passengers of his.

"Yes, yes," the old man said in accented English, nodding and smiling.

Although the old couple had been in America for seven or eight years, their English was still at the "yes and no," "good and bad" level. Their daughter had been urging them to spend more time learning English, but they kept pushing the excuse that they were too old to remember. Each time Tony saw them, he wanted to chat a little more but couldn't continue after a few words. Sometimes they didn't even nod at the appropriate moment. Fortunately, they could remember all the bus stops and had never made a mistake.

The church they were heading to was the most common kind in the western United States. If not for the cross on the roof and the stained-glass windows inlaid with the Virgin Mary, you'd think it was a large warehouse. Comparing them to Europe's majestic cathedrals with their magnificent towering spires, which had taken hundreds of years to build, it was doubtful how devout these Americans were. The good news was that they had many charitable programs, one of which was the free lunch open to the poor twice a week. Perhaps God could forgive them.

By the time the old couple arrived at the dining hall on the side of the church, panting heavily, the free lunch had been going on for some time. People had filled the rows of long tables. The various scents mingled together and pervaded the large room.

On the long table to the left of the entrance, there were pots of steaming-hot food. Several enthusiastic volunteers were busy behind the counter. Seeing them come in, Mary, with her curly red hair, grinned and said, "You're a little late today."

"Yes, yes." The old man nodded and reached across the table to get food from Mary.

His wife jabbed at him. "Don't take so many potatoes and bread," she whispered. "They're not worth anything."

"Okay, okay." As the old man proceeded in the line, he turned to survey the crowd. He was checking to see if Mrs. Shan Wang had come.

"Two servings of beef meatballs, please," his wife said in Chinese. In fact, she was telling her husband. She raised her index and middle fingers to the young man next to Mary and pointed to the meatballs in the pot.

Two servings was a lot. Seeing his wife's plate, the old man was a little embarrassed.

There were two groups of people who came regularly to eat the free lunch. One was homeless tramps who wore greasy clothes and exuded sour smells. They often sat in a corner and ate in silence. The other was old Chinese men and women, who ate, talked, and laughed loudly.

On the opposite side of the dining hall, Shan Wang saw the old man fetching foods at the entrance. She stood up and waved at him. The red scarf around her neck stood out.

The old man was about to walk over. His wife snatched him and pointed at the two seats close by with her lips. She then raised her face and shouted at Shan Wang, "We sit here today. Take your time."

The old man was a little glum. The wife grumbled, "Would you like to see her each time you come here?"

"What did you say? All of us are so old. Isn't it just talk?" said the old man.

"So many people here, and you only talk to her?" A hint of discontent seeped into her words.

The old man turned his head away to ignore her.

EARLY NEXT MORNING, Mr. Zhang, who lived on the same floor in the senior apartment building, called to tell them there were many fifty-percent-off sales at Jiuhua Supermarket today and asked whether they might want to run with him. The old couple was having breakfast. They'd brought back a pile of food from church yesterday, enough to eat for a while.

"Great, great," said the wife. "We'll be right there."

Still disturbed by his wife, the old man said, "Aren't you afraid I'll catch Shan Wang once more?"

"What's the matter with you?" Her voice rose.

The old man said nothing. At a time like this, he was always the first to concede.

Shoppers thronged the supermarket. Red and green tags decorated a wide range of discounted goods. The old people in the senior apartment had flocked here for bargains.

Fresh corn was seventy percent off. The seniors surrounded a big basket of corn. All around were the corn husks; the stripped and unwanted cores were thrown back into the basket. The staff of the grocery store ran after them to tidy up.

The old man's cell phone rang. It was his daughter. "How's Mom? You said she had a heart problem last night. Do you need me to take her to a doctor?"

The old man said, "No, no, it's all right this time. She ate too many meatballs yesterday."

"Okay, have a good rest. I'm very busy at the company these days."

The old man said, "We are shopping in the grocery store. There are many things marked down today. We've bought a lot."

"What can I say about you guys? You could kill yourselves. It's crazy!" the daughter said, unrestrained outrage in her voice.

When the old couple got back home with a cart full of groceries, Professor Liang had been standing by the door waiting for them for some time. He was their hourly care worker and arrived at ten o'clock sharp every morning. For poor people in this age group, the government paid for an hourly care worker for each family.

Mr. Liang had been a professor at a university in a coastal city in China. In his late sixties, he was of medium height and a little bald. If no one told you, it'd be hard to see he was once a college professor.

"Two old leaders went shopping again." Mr. Liang smiled. His voice was loud.

In China, the old man and his wife used to be leaders. One had been a deputy director, and the other a branch manager. This was how Mr. Liang had called them when he had first come here to work. First, they were a dozen years older than him. Second, it was true that they had been leaders. There was no harm in being charming.

The door opened. It was an ordinary little flat for seniors, with a living room and a bedroom, plus a kitchen and a bathroom. Mr. Liang kept the place clean and tidy throughout. He took the big bags of food and stuffed them into the fridge one by one.

He said with some concern, "Old leader, can't buy any more. The fridge is full. I have to put the two bags of bread you brought back yesterday outside."

"Okay, okay. You figure it out. Everything is up to you," said the old man.

Since Mr. Liang had come six months ago, the old man had been more relaxed. Although Mr. Liang had done little housework back in China, he had become proficient in recent years. The old couple sang the praises of the excellent southern Chinese dishes he cooked. For Mr. Liang, his wages of over ten dollars an hour were gratifying. He'd earn more than thirty dollars a morning doing light work while chatting with the old couple. So, he was serious about his work.

In the kitchen, Mr. Liang was cooking lunch.

The old couple turned on the TV and sat down on the armchairs on either side of the coffee table. The old man always let his wife choose whatever she wanted to watch. Recently, she'd been obsessed with Chinese financial programs. The red and green numbers on the screen often made her very excited.

"Mr. Liang, do you buy stocks?" she cried to the kitchen.

"I dare not!" Lao Liang answered, sticking his head out of the kitchen. "The money we have at our age is our life savings," he added.

"I mean with the pension money in China," said the wife.

Mr. Liang stepped out of the kitchen and raised his index finger to his mouth, signaling her to be quiet. The wife covered her mouth.

He grasped a bunch of Chinese chives and sat down.

While picking the chives, he said, "America's national welfare lets us have no worries!"

The wife said with emotion, "Yeah! When you're old, getting ill is the greatest fear. Not here. No cost for us to see a doctor. It's worry-free!" She grinned from ear to ear and then added, "Plus, with more than a thousand dollars in cash allowance for both of us, we couldn't possibly spend it all."

Everyone laughed.

The wife said, "The children are unreliable. I didn't expect to get adopted by a 'caring mother' when I got old."

The old man glanced at his wife. "Could we have come here without our daughter to help us with immigration?" he argued.

"Obviously not," the wife admitted.

"If that's the case," said Mr. Liang, "you can buy stocks with your pension savings in China." He added at once, "You have to decide for yourself. Don't take my word for it." Then he got the chives and returned to the kitchen.

After a while, several delicious dishes came to the table. Mr. Liang spent the rest of his time cleaning the rooms. Last, he picked up trash and finished his work for the day.

"Mr. Liang, would you like to stay for lunch? We bought a lot of stuff," the old man asked warmly.

"No, no," said Mr. Liang, "I'll be working at Boss Chen's home upstairs later."

The Boss Chen whom Mr. Liang alluded to had run a company before coming to the States. Everyone followed suit and called him the boss.

"I heard his son came yesterday and they had a big fight about something," the wife cut in.

"I heard," said Mr. Liang. "They had an awful quarrel. The son uttered cruel words, saying he won't recognize them as his parents." Then, Mr. Liang added, "It seems to be about calling 911."

The wife remembered something and said, "No wonder I saw the ambulance coming yesterday."

Mr. Liang leaned close to them and whispered, "In fact, Boss Chen was not that ill, except that his blood pressure was a little high. He didn't want to bother his son or pay for a taxi, just dialed 911. It's fast and free."

The old man said, "There is a discount for seniors to take a taxi. Isn't it just a few dollars?"

"Yeah," Mr. Liang said, "that's the reason his son was so furious. The hospital notified his son soon after the ambulance arrived yesterday. The son felt his parents are too absurd."

"If they do this kind of thing a few more times, nobody will come to save us in case of a real emergency next time," the old man said in an anxious voice.

HIS WIFE GREW MORE confident after watching the financial programs for a few days.

The Chinese stock market had soared for several days in a row, and many stocks triggered the daily circuit breaker. His wife couldn't sit still any longer. She regretted not doing it sooner.

A few days ago, her son had called from China to say that the hundreds of thousands of yuan in their retirement CD account had matured and asked if they were going to extend it for the same term length. The wife told her son that since the money had no use for the time being, she might as well buy stocks.

Yesterday her son had called and said he had put all the money into stock funds. From now on, she was doing it with live ammunition. The red and green numbers on the screen had an inseparable association with her now.

The old man kept asking his wife whether it was rational to play the stock market at this age, but she always pointed to a gathering of old people in the trading hall on the TV screen and said it was her age that gave her time to play with stocks, which also exercised her brain to avert dementia. No chance he could sway her.

A week passed. Another week of the surging Chinese stock market had left the wife feeling elated. Recently, she would pull Mr. Liang aside and describe to him the boom of the stock market, making Mr. Liang more or less remorseful. Still, Mr. Liang kept reminding her that the stock market was risky!

The old man could do nothing about it. As long as she was happy…

The market run-up that lasted for so many days in a row came to an abrupt end on Monday, as if a switch had been flipped. On the TV screen, the red numbers (red for up and green for down in China) vanished in a titanic market reversal. Everything turned into a dark gloom. The market rout continued on Tuesday and Wednesday. The old man changed the channel to prevent his wife from staring at the screen.

"Do you want to die? Don't you always say we have enough money? How dare you jump into the Chinese stock market most people shunned? At our age you…" The old man, seeing his wife not talking, felt he wasn't picking the right words. So, he stopped decrying her actions and decided to console her. "We have the national welfare. Just let it go if we lost money."

In this family, his wife's mood was of the utmost importance.

THE PEOPLE LIVING in the senior apartment seldom got letters. However, every unit had received a letter recently from the Social Security Administration.

The old couple couldn't understand a word in the letter. They called their daughter for a visit. The daughter said she was swamped and would come over on the weekend. She reminded them they could get Mr. Liang to help read it first. No one in this building could speak English better than Mr. Liang.

At ten o'clock in the morning, Mr. Liang brought up the letter as soon as he came in. He said he had also gotten one.

The old man pulled out the letter and asked Mr. Liang to explain it to them word for word. Mr. Liang put on his reading glasses and sat down. His mood appeared somewhat somber.

The letter went something like this, "Now it's time to renew your application for US national welfare benefits. Within a month, you must submit account information for all banks in the United States, and report the amount of your retirement pension in your country of origin. Otherwise, you will be disqualified from receiving benefits in the United States."

The wife was appalled yet soon calmed down. She knew very well that the two of them had just a single US bank account with a few hundred dollars in it. They had locked most of their cash, which amounted to tens of thousands of dollars, in a crate at home. In fact, the seniors here all knew they wouldn't get national welfare if their US bank deposits exceeded two thousand dollars.

"Mr. Liang, please speak more slowly. What about the pension you mentioned?" the wife interrupted. Her voice was a little dismayed.

Lao Liang repeated the sentence he had just read.

"What if we don't report our pension income in China?" The old man tried to control his voice. He knew he and his wife had never declared their monthly pension of around $1,700 in China. Many Chinese seniors accepting welfare benefits here never reported it either, as they were aware that if the US government found out someone had additional pension income in China, their welfare benefits would be revoked.

"If you deliberately conceal pension income in your country of origin"—Lao Liang's voice trembled—"and receive welfare from the federal government by fraudulent means, you could be sentenced to six months' imprisonment, which also jeopardizes your immigration status in the United States. This decision cannot be appealed."

The shrill sirens of the ambulance were fast approaching, and the ambulance soon stopped at the entrance of the senior apartment. The red and blue lights on its rooftop alternately hit the walls of the apartment building.

The old man sat stupefied by his unconscious wife. Turbid tears rolled down his wrinkled cheeks.

He mumbled, "National welfare, national welfare…"

缺席

~

出租车离开机场已经十分钟了,培兰还没有想好今晚住在哪里。十几个小时的国际航程,一分钟也没合眼,这会儿真的累了。她告诉司机,就在城中心随便找个旅店,不要太贵就行。

这次回来不同往常,一堆糟心的事情要处理。临走时老公一再交待培兰:这么远去一趟不容易。不要心软,快刀斩乱麻。

车快到市中心时,培兰改变了主意。她决定先去医院。市立医院离市中心不远,没绕多少路。她告诉司机,在医院对面的停车场等她二十分钟,她会加付这二十分钟的钱。司机说没问题。

市医院的住院部永远是最挤的地方。这次回来,培兰感觉比前些年更挤了。甚至走廊、楼梯口都加了床位。药水味,各种食物的混杂味,让人感觉这儿像是战场的后方医院。等她小心地侧过身子,让过床铺、陪床的家属和忙碌的护理,好不容易找到病房,已经十分钟过去了。

四个床位的病房里住得满满的。床与床之间用乳白色的帘子隔开。培兰走进房间,一个个挨着找。在最里面靠窗的床位上,看到了正睡着的公公。

隔壁陪床的老太太上下打量着培兰后,问,你是来看老张的?培兰说,我是他的儿媳妇,刚下飞机。老太太说,他的孙女刚刚离开,给老爷子送了些吃的来。培兰一惊,靠近老太太小声说,他只有一个孙子,哪儿来的孙女?老太太说,那就奇怪了。那个女孩自己说的。老太太又说,我看他们挺像爷孙俩。我还直夸她孝顺呢。自从老爷子住院,没见到其他人来过。

培兰不说话了,她已经猜到了八九不离十。这次回来,就是来斩这堆乱麻的。

三月的南方阴冷阴冷的,没有一点春天的样子。树枝上的苞蕾缩得紧紧的,显出了一种对春天的失望。

昨天培兰没等公公醒来,就急忙从医院里出来了。

旅途的疲劳让她一到旅店就睡下了,一直到这会儿,才从乱七八糟的睡梦中醒来。她要让大脑好好休息休息,以便清楚地理顺这次回来要面对的事情。

这次本应是培兰的老公张诚回来的,这些都是他家的事。可是张诚已经和父亲断绝联系快半年了,他说他不能原谅父亲,宁愿不要家里财产。但是培兰不愿意。张诚是他们唯一的儿子。今后他的父母走了,做儿子的理应得到财产。没有什么道理好讲。然而，怎么处理这些事，培兰心里还是没有底。

起床后，培兰按照国内的习惯把自己好好收拾了一下。平时在美国随便惯了，松松垮垮的棉质衣服，一双运动鞋，头发随意绾在脑后。这次她特意买了几件比较时髦的衣服，临来时还花了些钱，把头发烫成现在国内中年妇女流行的样子。

这次回国，除了自己随身物品，培兰只带了一个名牌手提包。这是她为她的一个同学准备的一份礼物。大学毕业后，这个同学改行做了律师。培兰有些问题要向她咨询，有必要的话，还要请她出庭打官司。

早晨，天气还像昨天一样湿冷。太阳隐隐约约地斜挂在天上，让人看不出是晴天还是阴天。

上班的高峰过了。培兰弯到旅馆后街的一家小笼包子店。每次她和老公回来，都要来这家店。同样是猪肉馅子做的包子，这儿的就是香。回美国就再也吃不到这种纯正的味道了。

在这个时段里，饭店里没有太多的人。培兰挑了一个角落坐了下来，点了每次必点的几样：一笼小笼包子，一碗鸡汤和一小碟糖醋花生米。她慢慢地吃着，静静地想着。

以前培兰回国都是和张诚一起，每次也都是住张诚家。这次她一个人回来，走之前也没有通知公公婆婆。如果公公没住院，一切还能按原计划进行。可是，几天前公公近似自杀的行为让所有的计划都泡汤了。现在不管做什么，似乎都不太近人情。

培兰和张诚结婚后，只和他的父母住了几个月就出国了。在美国的二十年里,老俩口曾去住过两次,每次时间都不长。培兰和张诚也回来过几次。由于没有很多假期,每次都是来去匆匆。五年前婆婆的一次中风,造成了半边瘫痪。从那时起,家里开始雇了保姆。

培兰见过她。那时她二十出头,初中毕业。虽然来自农村,但没有农村人的模样,皮肤白皙,身材匀称,举止得体,话也不多。培兰第一次看到她时是在冬天。她穿着一条黑裤配一件枣红色的宽领羊毛衫;另一次是在夏天,她穿着一条浅灰色的的薄裤,上面是一件白梨花粉红底的短袖,让人看着很舒服。

她的名字叫梨花。

培兰和公公婆婆相处的时间不多。公公是那种没有脾气,话也不多的人。除了研究所的工作,在家里还承担了一多半的家务。他对婆婆的任何行为都能容忍。以至于培兰经常向张诚发牢骚,为什么你就不像你爸。

梨花做了保姆没多久,公公就把家里大部分的事都交给了她,包括买菜,去医院拿药,甚至去银行取钱存钱。

张诚渐渐地发现,以前常常提起让他们回国的父亲,很久不提这个事了。这本是张诚的一块心病。父母不愿意来美国,年纪越来越大的他们又得不到照顾。特别是每次回国,亲戚、邻里都向自己善意地唠叨。这种压力常让他透不过气来。梨花的出现,让全家觉得有了依靠。那种无形的压力似乎慢慢地得到了释放。

可是梨花来了两年之后,情况发生了变化。一次张诚妈妈打来电话。从她含糊不清的话语中,张诚了解到已经退休的父亲包揽了所有的家务。梨花只有在周末的两天才干活。平时从周一到周五都是早出晚归。张诚问父亲,为什么要这样安排?父亲说自己退休后不那么忙了，梨花只要做两天就够了。当时张诚觉得合理，就没有深究。只是又问，为什么梨花平时晚上还要住在家里？父亲含含糊糊地解释，她在别人家做钟点工，没地方住，暂住在家里。后来，还是张诚的小姨了解到真相。原来这几年父亲一直在资助梨花上学。半年前梨花中专毕业时，父亲还帮她找到了工作。

没有人能理解父亲为什么要这样做。张诚也不想把父亲想得那么糟糕。可是张诚就是想不通，为什么他要背着母亲去资助一个无亲无故的保姆。难怪小姨在电话里说了那么多难听话。小姨告诉张诚，这种事太多了：主人有外遇，小保姆卷走家中的财产……张诚无论如何不相信父亲是那种人。他一直和小姨争辩，直到有一天小姨打来电话，用鄙夷的声音告诉他，她和姨夫在购物中心看见梨花挽着父亲的胳膊。她说父亲对不起生病的母亲，说了很多难听的话。

张诚愤怒了！他怎么也没想到，从小敬重的父亲会做出这种难以启齿的事情。那一夜，他彻底无眠。

第二天，他想用攒够的勇气给父亲打电话。他要质问父亲，为什么？为什么在晚年要伤害家人，而且是用这种方式。最终，电话没有打过去。他找不出任何合适的词语去质问年迈的父亲，特别是在这种事情上。

时间快近中午，饭店里的人渐渐多了起来；已经有人开始排队等位子了。培兰站了起来，她决定还是先去医院。不管从情理上还是从道义上，都应该再去看看公公。

马路上人来人往，开始热闹起来。放学的孩子们成群结队、叽叽喳喳地从培兰身边走过；上班的人也在这个时间出来吃午饭。城市中熙来攘往的声音赶走了空气中的凉意。

培兰每次回来，都喜欢在人多的街道上走上几个来回，好让这久违的人气驱散掉积累已久的孤独感。这次却并没有找到这种感觉。她有些后悔这次的仓促行动。

医院病房正在发放午餐。拿着碗盘的病人和家属们把走廊堵得水泄不通。培兰等了一会儿，让过拥挤的人群，来到病房。

房间尽头，公公面对着窗户呆坐着。床边柜子上放着刚买来的饭菜。他眼神黯然，眼睑低垂。凌乱的白发向一边支楞着，看上去倍显沧桑。培兰在他身后站了一会儿，他浑然无觉。当培兰在他的对面坐了下来时，他稍稍一惊，但很快眼神又暗淡下去。他轻声说，你来了？培兰点点头说，昨天到的。您还好吗？他没有回答，转身拿起床头柜上的饭，把头压得低低的，一小口一小口地吃了起来。公公平时话就少。在这种情况下，培兰真的不知道应该说什么。

护士进来打针，打破了沉默。她一再叮嘱，老年人不能受凉，特别是在春天。

空气有些凝重。培兰悄悄地退了出来。

出了医院大门，她迎面碰到匆匆往里走的梨花。梨花先是一楞，然后笑了笑说，阿姨回来了。

从她的眼神中培兰看不出任何不安、羞愧和懊悔，俨然就像孙女去看爷爷。她说，午饭时间过来看看，晚上再来陪爷爷。她还说，如果培兰有时间，想一起好好聊一聊爷爷的情况。

. . .

晚上，在离医院不远的咖啡厅里，梨花坐在培兰的对面。

忽隐忽现的烛光落在梨花略显苍白的脸上，让培兰觉得梨花比她第一次见到时要苍老、憔悴不少。这几年功夫，她像是从一个羞涩的少女变成了一个成熟的少妇。

梨花很熟练地点了一些甜点，又给自己点了一杯咖啡。培兰要了一杯矿泉水，因为她晚上不能喝咖啡。

梨花很大方地坐在那里，好像要告诉培兰一个别的女孩和另一个爷爷的故事。

她说得很平静。

梨花说，上个星期天下午，姨夫突然来找爷爷。他进门就板着脸。样子让人看了喘不过气来。他和爷爷关在卧室里，说要进行一次男人之间的对话。在这半小时里，我只能约莫听到姨夫断断续续的声音，中间常常有几分钟的停顿。静得让人有些害怕。等他们出来的时候，我看见爷爷像是被抽掉内脏的空壳，呆站在那里。我问他发生了什么事。他动了动嘴唇，稳了稳慌乱的表情。突然，近似吼的声音从他嗓子里喊了出来：耻辱！放屁！声音大得远不像平时，犹如用攒了一辈子的力气，说出了可能是他这一辈子说的最难听的话。

那天晚上在淋浴间，爷爷用冰冷的水足足冲了二十分钟。第二天就发起了高烧。他想用这种自残的行为，来抗议加在自己身上的耻辱。因为烧得很高，爷爷下午就住进了医院。

梨花继续说，爷爷住院的当天晚上，我去找了小姨夫。小姨夫严肃地警告我，不要有非分之想。小姨还问我骗了你们家多少钱，还说要去告我。

梨花很夸张地笑了一下，笑得十分苦涩。接着张开嘴，昂起头，可是眼眶中的眼泪没能停止下落。她啜泣起来，是特别酸楚的那种声音。

培兰递过纸巾。梨花擦去眼泪后勉强地笑了一下。她清了清嗓子想继续说下去，可是声音抖得不行。她拿起杯子一点一点啜着咖啡，想努力稳定一下情绪。过了一会，她昂起头提高了嗓音说，其实在这个家里没有人了解爷爷，更没有人关心他。你们知道吗？他已经得忧郁症近十年了。你们出国后他生活得很孤独。奶奶的病和退休更加重了他的病情。

培兰很吃惊。这是她没有想到的。她想知道后面又发生了什么。

梨花接着说，我想先说说我自己，这样你可能会更理解爷爷所做的一些事情。

你们可能已经知道，我原来有个家，现在只剩下我自己了。我爸妈在我和哥哥很小的时候就去南方打工了。头几年里，每到过年，他们都还拎着大包小包回来看我们，但后来就不回来了。听奶奶说，我爸妈离婚后又各自在南方城市成立了自己的小家。哥哥比我大五岁，也是早早就去城里打工。他取了媳妇后也不回来了。爷爷很早就死了，农村的家只剩下我和奶奶。那一阵子，因为生气，奶奶病了很久。我向奶奶发誓，一定要好好读书，考上大学，在城里找个好工作，把奶奶接到城里去。从那以后，奶奶不再让我干农活了，要我专心学习。我们俩就像一个团队。

说到这里，梨花停了一下。她深深地吸了一口气继续说，有一天奶奶从镇上卖完鸡蛋回来，当她走在半道时，正遇到劈头盖脸的雷暴雨。空旷的田野上，她躲也没处躲，一个闪电正好打在她头天忘在裤兜里的铁顶针箍上。被抬回来的时候，她的半条腿都烧焦了。我失去了奶奶，也失去了生活的来源。

这一段话，梨花说得比培兰想象的要坚强。可是培兰不行了。她去了一趟洗手间，回来时两眼通红。

梨花继续说，自从有一天我告诉爷爷我的一切后，爷爷比以前更沉默了。有一阵子，他连饭都吃不下去。记得那一天，他突然说要资助我去上学。我吓坏了，坚持要他去看医生。

在医生那里，爷爷被诊断为重度忧郁症。其实爷爷在这之前就已经生病了。之后我们又去看了一个心理医生，在网上查了很多有关资料，最后制订了一套治疗忧郁症的方案。

此刻，梨花脸上露出些微笑。她接着说，心理医生告诉我们，对于一个忧郁症患者来说，在繁忙的商店里坐上一个小时，喝点饮料，看着人群来来往往，要比坐在孤寂的家里更有利于身心的恢复，因为这些人没有可以依赖的内在的快乐源泉。

梨花开始兴奋起来。她拿起杯子喝了一大口咖啡说，从那以后，我一有时间就陪爷爷坐在咖啡店里看着人来人往，或者在大街上走来走去。这些都是给爷爷治病的。

培兰问，奶奶知道吗？

没有人知道。梨花说，爷爷不让我告诉任何人他得了忧郁症。说句实话，奶奶从不关心他；你们的小姨和小姨夫也很冷漠。这些年，虽然他的日子过得很凄凉，但他不想再去打扰你们，把一切都闷在心里。

爷爷资助我上学的事也是医生支持的。医生说，很多忧郁症病人对于生活在自己身边的人的苦难和不幸倍感难过。如果帮助别人能让他们有一种被需要的感觉，即肯定了自己的价值，又解决了别人的困难，他们的身体里就会释放出快乐的元素。在医生的鼓励下，我接受了爷爷的资助。

故事的碎片一点点缝合了。

培兰内心涌出了难以形容的羞愧和不安。我们差一点轻率地伤害了一个本应感激的人。人性能有多美好、多善良，就能有多阴暗、多丑恶。这么多年自己和张诚一直在美国打拼，没有关心自己的亲人，让他们在凄凉的晚年里，抑郁寡欢、闷闷不乐地打发日子。

培兰理解公公了。当疾病、衰老和孤独吞噬着他的生命时，他做出来的举动或许是惊人的。

梨花看似漫不经心却非常刻意地对倍兰说，小姨他们说我想要爷爷家的财产。你们放心，爷爷资助我上学，又帮我找到了工作，这是我最大的财富。我很幸运！她的眼神蓦然变得很凌厉。她向培兰一字一句地说，我不会拿你们家的财产。如果今后你们不能回来，我将为爷爷奶奶养老送终。

回到旅店，培兰把所有一切都告诉了张诚。

电话那边，张诚沉默了很久。懊悔、羞辱和愤怒杂陈。他深深地吸了一口气，像是在水里闷了很久。他告诉培兰，现在就订回国的机票。他还说，想在国内找一个工作机会。他更想告诉父亲，生命中的温暖和爱也许会因为某些原因迟到，但决不能缺席，永远不能！

第二天是周末。培兰和梨花约好一起去看公公。她还要把那个漂亮的名牌手提包送给梨花。

THE ABSENCE

∼

*I*t had been ten minutes since the taxi had left the airport, but Pelan hadn't figured out where to stay for the night. She hadn't gotten a wink of sleep during the over-ten-hour international voyage, and she was feeling tired. She asked the driver to please find a hotel in the center of the city, as long as it wasn't too expensive.

This trip differed from the usual ones before; Pelan had a load of vexed things to deal with. When she'd left home, her husband had nagged her a few times: "It's hard to make a long trip. Don't be softhearted. Cut the Gordian knot."

As the car approached downtown, Pelan changed her mind. She wanted to go to the hospital first. The municipal hospital was near the city center. She asked the driver to wait twenty minutes in the parking lot opposite the hospital, and she'd pay for the extra time. The driver said no problem.

THE INPATIENT DEPARTMENT of the hospital was always the most crowded place. Pelan felt it was even more crowded than in previous years. There were beds added in the corridors and stairwells. The medicinal aroma, mixed with all kinds of food smells, made the place feel like a field hospital in a combat zone. She made her way carefully through the sickbeds, patients' acquaintances, nurses, and shelves. By the time she found the ward, ten minutes had passed.

The four-bed ward was full. A milky-white drape separated the beds from each other. She walked into the room and looked at the beds one by one. At last, she saw her father-in-law sleeping on the innermost bed by the window.

An old lady sitting by the next bed looked her up and down and asked, "Are you here to see Mr. Zhang?"

"I'm his daughter-in-law, just got off the plane," said Pelan.

The old lady said, "His granddaughter just left. She brought food."

Surprised, Pelan drew closer to the old lady and whispered, "He has only one grandson. Where did the granddaughter come from?"

The old lady said, "That's weird. The girl said it herself. I see them like grandpa and granddaughter." She added, "I even praised her filial piety. I've seen nobody else since he came here."

Having guessed what was going on, Pelan stopped talking. This was the reason she had come back—to clean up the mess.

IT WAS a chilly March in southern China. The flower buds on the tree branches shrank tightly to show their disappointment in the late-coming spring.

Pelan had hurried out of the hospital yesterday without waiting for her father-in-law to wake up.

The weariness from traveling allowed her to fall asleep as soon as she'd checked into the hotel, and only now did she wake up from a series of confused dreams.

She needed a good rest, so she could have a clear picture of what she was about to confront.

Cheng Zhang, Pelan's husband, should have returned this time, knowing these troubles were all his family's business. However, Cheng had cut contact with his father nearly six months earlier, saying he could not forgive his father and would rather give up the family assets. But Pelan wasn't willing to surrender. Cheng was their only son and deserved to inherit the assets left by his parents. There shouldn't be any doubt. However, she was uncertain how to deal with the headache.

After getting up, Pelan tidied herself up according to the custom in China. She had been casual in the States, often wearing baggy cotton clothes and a pair of sneakers, with her hair loosely tied back. Not this time, though. She had purposely brought a few fashionable garments and also spent money perming her hair to copy the trend among the middle-aged women in China.

Besides her belongings, Pelan had bought a designer handbag before coming. It was the only gift she'd purchased for one of her classmates, who had changed course after college to become a lawyer. Pelan had legal questions and might even ask her friend to appear in court for a lawsuit if needed.

THE WEATHER WAS STILL as cold and wet as yesterday morning. The sun hung faintly in the sky, making it hard to tell whether it was sunny or cloudy.

After the rush hour, Pelan went to a steamed dumpling shop behind the hotel. She came to this place each time she returned to China with her husband. The pork-filled steamed dumplings here were so much tastier and more authentic than those found in the States.

There were few people in the eatery. Palin took a seat in a corner. She ordered the same thing she got every time: a steamer basket of dumplings, a bowl of chicken soup, and a small plate of sweet-and-sour peanuts. She ate while pondering.

In the past, Pelan had come back with Cheng and stayed at his parents' place. This time, she was by herself and hadn't let her parents-in-law know she was coming. If her father-in-law hadn't been in the hospital, she'd have carried everything out according to her original plan. However, his suicide attempt a few days back had caused all her plans to fizzle out. No matter what they did now, it would make them look stingy and mean.

After Pelan and Cheng had gotten married, they'd only lived with his parents for a few months before they had gone aboard. In the past twenty years, the old couple had visited them in the States twice but hadn't stayed long either time. Pelan and Cheng had also come back several times. Since there weren't many holidays, they'd come and gone in a hurry. Five years ago, her mother-in-law had suffered a stroke that had left her paralyzed on one side. The family had hired a caregiver since then.

Pelan had met her before. She was in her early twenties and had finished her middle school. Although she was from the countryside, she didn't seem like a rural girl. She was fair-skinned, well-proportioned, and quiet, with decent manners. The first time Pelan had seen her was in winter. She had worn a pair of black trousers with a wide-neck maroon sweater; another time was in summer, and she had worn thin light gray pants and a short-sleeved pink shirt with white pear flowers, giving a pleasant impression.

Her name was Lihua.

Pelan hadn't spent much time with her parents-in-law. Cheng's father was a mild-mannered person of few words. Besides his job at a research institute, he shouldered the greater part of the family chores. He could tolerate any conduct from his wife. So much so that Pelan had often grumbled to Cheng, asking why he disliked his dad.

Not long after Lihua had become their caregiver, the father-in-law had handed over most of the family's responsibilities to her, including buying groceries, going to the hospital's pharmacy, and even heading off to the bank to withdraw or deposit cash.

Cheng had gradually discovered that his dad, who had often told him to return to China, never mentioned it again after Lihua came. It had been a big concern for Cheng that his parents, who didn't want to come to the States, wouldn't be taken care of as they got older. Especially when they returned home, relatives and neighbors kept on pestering them. Their intentions were good, but the pressure they applied was unbearable. Lihua made the whole family feel they could depend on her, which helped to release the invisible weight.

However, the situation had changed after two years. Once, Cheng's mother had called. From her vague words, Cheng had learned that his father, who had retired, had assumed almost all the housework duties. Lihua only worked on the weekends. She'd head out early and return late during the weekdays. Cheng had asked his father, "Why do you want this arrangement?" His father had said he wasn't so occupied after retirement, and having Lihua here for two days would be sufficient. Cheng had found that explanation reasonable and hadn't delved into it any further. Just asked, "Why does Lihua still sleep in your home every night?" His father explained vaguely that she was working in someone's house during the day and had nowhere to stay for the time being. Later, it was Cheng's aunt who'd learned the truth. It turned out his father had been helping her to go to school. When she'd graduated from the secondary vocational school six months ago, his father had even helped her to find a job.

No one understood why his father had done it. Cheng wouldn't like to consider that his father might be a bad person. However, he couldn't make sense of why his father was supporting an unrelated caregiver without getting his mother involved. No wonder his aunt had said those nasty words on the phone. These things happened all the time, she said. An old man had an affair with his young caregiver, who later ran off with the family's assets... Cheng didn't believe his father was that kind of person. He had argued with her about it, until one day, she'd called again to let him know in a disdainful voice that she and Uncle had seen Lihua holding his father's arm in a shopping center. "Your father betrayed your sick mother," said she. More nasty words followed.

Cheng was furious! He'd never thought his respected father would do such an unspeakable thing. That night, he didn't sleep at all.

The following day, he tried to muster enough courage to call his father. He wanted to ask, "Why? Why harm your family this way, and so late in life?" He didn't call since he couldn't find any suitable words to interrogate his elderly father, especially in such matters.

IT WAS ALMOST NOON, and the restaurant had become more crowded; a line had formed. Pelan got up and decided to go to the hospital first. It didn't feel right not to see her father-in-law once more.

The streets were bustling with people. The school children passed by her in droves, chattering loudly. Office workers were also out for lunch. The noise of the city drove away the chill in the air.

Each time Pelan came back, she liked to walk up and down the crowded streets a few times so the long-lost hustle and bustle of people would dispel her accrued loneliness. Not this time. She regretted her hasty trip.

In the hospital ward, lunch meals were being passed out. Patients and family members with bowls and plates jammed the hallway. Pelan waited for a while to yield to the crowd before stepping in the ward.

At the end of the room, her father-in-law sat facing the window. There was a fresh lunch tray on the bedside cabinet. His eyes were dim, eyelids drooping. His unkempt white hair spiked to one side, revealing the vicissitudes of his life. He was oblivious to Pelan observing him from behind. When Pelan sat down opposite him, he was a little startled, but soon his eyes were dim again. He mumbled, "You are here?"

Pelan nodded and said, "I arrived yesterday. Are you all right?"

Without answering, he turned to pick up his lunch, and with his head bowed, he started eating, one small bite at a time. Her father-in-law had never been talkative. Pelan didn't know what to say either under the circumstances.

The nurse came in and broke the silence. Old people

should avoid catching a cold, she repeated, particularly in spring.

The air was a little heavy. Pelan slipped out.

At the hospital entrance, she ran into Lihau, who was rushing in. She was bewildered for a second, then smiled and said, "Auntie, you are back."

Pelan could see no uneasiness, shame, or remorse in her eyes. It was much the same as a grandchild going to a grandpa. She said she'd come and take a look at lunchtime and then come back to spend the evening with Grandpa. She also said that if Pelan had time, she'd like a good chat about Grandpa's situation.

THAT NIGHT, in the coffee shop close to the hospital, Lihau sat across from Pelan.

The glimmering candlelight fell on her pale face, making Lihua look older and more gaunt than the first time Pelan had seen her. She appeared to have transformed from a shy girl into a mature young lady in recent years.

Lihua quickly ordered some sweets, and then a cup of coffee for herself. Pelan asked for a glass of mineral water as she didn't drink coffee during the evening.

Lihua sat there with ease, as though preparing to reveal an account of some other woman and another grandpa.

She spoke calmly.

"Last Sunday afternoon, Uncle came to see Grandpa out of the blue. He came in with a straight face. His manner would make one breathless to look at him. They locked themselves in the bedroom and said there would be a conversation between men. For half an hour, I could only hear Uncle's intermittent voice, and there were often pauses that lasted a few minutes. The silence was a little frightening. When they came out, I saw Grandpa standing there like an empty shell. I asked him what had happened. He moved his lips and steadied himself, a frantic expression on his face. Suddenly, a roar left his throat. 'Shame on you! Bullshit!' His voice was far from normal, as if he had uttered what might have been the most unpleasant words he had ever said, using strength he'd refrained from using his entire life.

"That night, Grandpa took a twenty-minute-long ice-cold shower. He became ill with a high fever following day. His self-harm was a protest against the humiliation other people inflicted on him. Because of his high temperature, he was admitted to the hospital in the afternoon."

Lihua continued, "That evening, I went to see Uncle. He sternly warned me not to have wild desires. Aunt also asked me how much money I had cheated your family out of. She said she would sue me."

Lihau gave an exaggerated and bitter grin. At that point, she opened her mouth and held her head up, yet she couldn't stop the tears in her eyes from falling. She sobbed in a distressed voice.

Pelan passed her a tissue. Lihua wiped away the tears, then reluctantly smiled. She cleared her throat, but her voice was too shaky to continue. Trying to steady her emotions, she picked up her cup and slowly sipped coffee. After a while, she raised her head and her voice. In fact, she said,

"No one in this family understood Grandpa or cared about him. Guess what? He had been suffering from depression for almost ten years. His life was very lonely after you and Uncle went abroad. Grandma's illness and his retirement had aggravated his condition."

Pelan was astonished. This was something she hadn't considered at all. She wanted to know what had happened next.

"I want to talk about myself first," Lihua said, "so you may understand what Grandpa did for me.

"As you may already know, I used to have a home, and now I am left alone. My parents went to work in the south when my brother and I were young. In the first few years, they came back to see us with their oversized bags every Spring Festival. But then they stopped coming. According to my grandma, they divorced and set up their own separate families in the southern city. My brother is five years older than me, and he also went to the city to work years ago. He'd never come back after he got married. My grandpa died young. Grandma and I were the only ones left in the countryside. For quite a while, Grandma was sick as a result of the outrage. I swore to Grandma that I'd study hard, go to college, find a good job in the city, and bring her with me. After that, Grandma wouldn't let me do any farmwork and asked me to concentrate on my studies. The two of us were like a team."

Lihua paused for a second, took a deep breath, and said, "One day, Grandma was coming back from selling her eggs in town. When she was halfway home, she was caught in a slashing thunderstorm while walking in an open field. There was no place to hide. A bolt of lightning hit the iron thimble she'd left in her pants pocket the day before and burnt half of her legs. I lost my grandma and my source of support."

As she told this story, Lihua was stronger than Pelan would have expected. However, Pelan wasn't as strong. She went to the restroom and came back red-eyed.

Lihua continued, "One day I told Grandpa all these things. Grandpa became more silent than before. For a while, he couldn't eat a bite. I remembered the day when he suddenly said that he was going to fund my education. I was scared and insisted he should see a doctor. At the doctor's office, Grandpa was diagnosed with severe depression. In fact, Grandpa had been ill before that. We then went to see a psychologist, looked up a lot of information on the internet, and drew up a plan to treat his depression."

A smile appeared on her face at that moment. Lihau added, "The psychologist let us know that for patients with depression, sitting for an hour in a busy shop to have a drink while watching the crowd might be more beneficial to their recovery than sitting in a lonely house, because these people have no inner source of happiness to depend on."

Lihua grew energized. She picked up the cup and took a long sip of coffee. "From that point on, we often sat in a coffee shop, watching people come and go. It was part of Grandpa's treatment."

"Did Grandma know this? said Pelan.

"No one knows," Lihua said. "Grandpa wouldn't let me tell anyone about his depression. To be honest, Grandma never cared about him. Your aunt and uncle are also extremely apathetic. Grandpa had been having a miserable life all these years, but he didn't want to bother you guys, so he kept everything to himself.

"The doctor also encouraged Grandpa to finance my school. Many people with depression, the doctor said, can be disheartened by the suffering and misfortune of those around them. If helping others can make them feel happy and needed, which affirms their own value by solving the difficulties of others, then their bodies will release the happy elements. With the doctor's encouragement, I accepted Grandpa's financial support."

The fragments of the story had come together bit by bit.

An indescribable shame and uneasiness welled up in Pelan's heart. *We almost inadvertently hurt a woman to whom we ought to be grateful. As beautiful and kind as human nature can be, it can also be dark and ugly on the flip side.* Over the years, we've been buckling down in the States, not caring about our loved ones, letting them spend their twilight years in sadness and despondency.

Pelan understood her father-in-law now. When illness, aging, and loneliness devoured his life, his actions might be confounding.

Lihua looked unconcerned when she said to Pelan, "Auntie said I want to grab Grandpa's assets. Please don't worry. It was my greatest fortune to have Grandpa help me go to school and find a job. I feel blessed." Her eyes suddenly became sharp. "I won't take your family's assets," she told Pelan. "If you guys can't come back, I'll nurse

Grandpa and Grandma throughout their remaining years, until the day when they leave this world."

BACK AT THE HOTEL, Pelan told Cheng everything.

On the other end of the phone, Cheng was silent. Remorse, shame, and anger mingled in him. He took a deep breath, as if his head had been underwater for a long time. He told Pelan he'd book a flight home immediately and try to find a job in China. He'd let his father know that warmth and love might come late in life but must not be absent —never!

The next day was a weekend. Pelan arranged to see her father-in-law together with Lihua. She also wanted to give Lihua the beautiful designer handbag.

夜宿

姚冰打过电话，又在艾琳家门前等了半个小时，还是不见她的人影。他心里想，现在的年青人怎么会这样，连做生意都不守时。网上的广告倒是吹得天花乱坠，什么环境清新优美，室内温馨舒适，各样用品齐全；像回到自己家一样。见鬼！姚冰骂了一句。回到自己家会连门都进不去吗？

他围着艾琳家的房子转了一圈，想看一看这里的环境到底是怎么个清新优美。

这里是一片典型的美国中产住的独立房。因为地处地皮昂贵的旧金山，每家院子都建得小巧玲珑。窗台上，栅栏里，精心布置的各种花卉，在温和宜人的好天气里竞相开放。

姚冰发现艾琳家的门前却没种什么花草。只有几棵仙人掌孤零零地杵在那里，旁边还有一些叫不出名字的植物，大概因为缺水，在阳光下岌岌可危。姚冰还发现,艾琳家建了两幢一模一样的房子,两房中间是铺上水泥的中院。他一时搞不清,这房子是属于一户人家还是两户。

又是十分钟过去了。姚冰真的不耐烦了。他想,这次一定要在网上给艾琳一个差评。

由于最近两年公司的生意不好,老板抠缩每一分钱。原来出差至少可以住上星级酒店,现在只让住六十美元以下的。妈的!六十美元能在旧金山这地方住上什么酒店?连打地铺都找不到。他寻来找去,只有住这种和别人合住的爱彼迎(Airbnb)。这种生意现在在全世界很流行,把自己家的房子通过网站出租给别人。合租便宜,单租就贵。姚冰当然只能选择合租。就好比只有几块钱还想吃餐馆?只能吃麦当劳了。

姚冰正想着,一辆红色的雷克萨斯冲上了房子的车道。

艾琳边开车门边大声地说,对不起!实在是对不起!让您久等了。真不巧,今天公司有个会议没能脱身。急匆匆的话语,伴随着高跟鞋敲打地面的声音一起来到姚冰的面前。接着,她又急匆匆地解释,这是从来没有发生过的事情。你应该能从以前的客人给我留下的评语中,了解到我的服务和为人。她说得顾影自怜,好像姚冰此刻正在给她写评语似的。要知道每个租客过后留下的评语对今后的生意至关重要。好生意都是冲着好评语来的。

这是一个年轻、姣好、又有些未老先衰的面容。淡淡的容妆上点缀着细细的汗珠。姚冰虽有气,但是真到了面前还是把积攒的牢骚咽了回去。

艾琳边开房门边说,明天我就叫人来安装电子数码门锁。今后我只要告诉你们门锁的密码就行了,也不会害得你等了这么久。说着，她又道了一番歉。

这是一幢两层楼的住宅。楼下的面积并不太大，客厅、餐厅和厨房能一眼看到头。厨房的台面上摆满了各种各样的中华料理，甚至连"老干妈"辣油都有，真是应了她的广告上说的各样用品齐全。看得出这里的客源主要是华人。客厅角落的墙边靠着一个高尔夫球杆袋。姚冰很喜欢打高尔夫，所以颇感兴趣。艾琳告诉他，这些球杆已经在这墙角歇息快二年了，每天忙得脚不着地，那有功夫娱乐和缎练身体。

艾琳从小和父母一起从大陆移民来美国。她的先生是在美国土生土长的华人。一聊起来，姚冰和艾琳还是半个老乡，都来自上海；这样两人一下就近乎了不少。艾琳临时决定，用同样的价钱，把姚冰的房间改换到楼上一间稍大一点的，不用和别人共用一个洗澡间。最后一点对姚冰很重要。和别人共用洗澡间还是他二十几年前刚来美国做学生时的住法。

所谓大一点的房间，也就是能摆一张床、一张桌子和一把椅子。姚冰悄悄地观察了一下。楼上有四间房间，加上楼下原本要租给他的那一间，一共五间。如果这些房间同时都租了出去，可就热闹了。他很久都没有过这种体验了。

安顿好姚冰，艾琳进了隔壁的房间。出来时，她已经换下了职业装，一身长裙衬着脸上重新加厚的浓妆。她匆匆闪过姚冰的门口，下楼，关门，在一阵汽车引擎和急踩油门的刺耳声中扬尘而去。

姚冰苦笑着摇了摇头。

手机响了，是老板萨婼的电话。这是姚冰最不愿意看到的。真他妈的见鬼！姚冰骂着。可是电话接通后，传过去的声音还是毕恭毕敬的。有什么办法呢？岁月已经磨练出了他的各种能力。

老板在电话里说，这次客户会议太重要了。如果能修复和他们的关系，谈成这笔生意，公司就有救了。你要做好充分的准备。慎重！慎重！再慎重！

从手机里出来的啰啰嗦嗦的声音，几乎淡出了姚冰的耳朵。这个老太太，你搞砸的事让我来擦屁股，你自己怎么不亲自来？姚冰心里骂着。

命运真是叵测难料。

来这家小公司四年里，姚冰感到日子过得就像走了一趟人间炼狱。原本在一家大公司干的好好的，领着一个不小的团队，获得上上下下的认可。一切都顺风顺水。然而，燕雀安知鸿鹄之志！他一拍脑袋辞职了。姚冰没有想到，自己踏上的是一条正在风雨中飘摇欲沉的破船。让他后悔的是，一开始没有认清这个萨婼。从表面上看，她算得上是一个温文尔雅的老太太；可实际上是个半阴半阳、心胸狭窄的掌控狂，且深谙世故，手眼通天。在她下面工作，姚冰一直被挟在板缝里，有劲使不上。每当公司有一个糟糕的季度，她总能把自己应负的责任推给下属。一不小心，不知道谁就会在浑然无觉中，被她抓了当替罪羊。唉！真是来找虐。

门外传来了一阵笑声。——是那种旁若无人的笑。这笑声随着推开的门滚入屋里，直冲楼上。姚冰皱了皱眉头，心想，一定是另外一拨房客回来了。

听声音是三个女人。第一个女人说，街对面站着的那个白人老头一直在盯着我看。我有那么好看吗？

另一个是有着很重东北腔的女人声音。她接着说，瞧你美的，今天你穿的裙子太性感了！连我都想多看你几眼。

第三个女人又对第一个女人说，他只看了你一眼，后来就一直盯着我看了。说完，三个女人一起哈哈地笑了起来。

姚冰正在修改明天要给客户的报告，瞬间思路就被打乱了。他想摔门，又觉得不妥，左手一用劲，右手又马上接住，然后再轻轻地掩上。他必须学会控制住自己。想想刚到公司的时候，自己是志得意满，甚至还有些自视甚高。可是和萨婼打了几个回合后，万事只求忍了。这是万全之策。沉浮荣辱都在身外，保住工作最重要。二个女儿目前都在上大学。

天渐渐晚了。一直在电脑上忙碌的姚冰感觉饿了。上一顿饭还是在飞机上吃的。他当时只买了一小块冰冷的三明治。连水都要自己掏钱。也难怪，自己坐的是那种最廉价的航线，这也是萨婼制定的新规定之一。想想那些年在大公司出差坐商务仓，心中不免泛起难言的失落。

姚冰出门去吃晚饭，迎面碰到了刚要进门的一对男女，听口音是从台湾来的。男的高而胖，略有些腆肚，花白的头发有些油腻；女的虽然年纪不小了，说起话来仍旧嗲声嗲气。还没说上两句，男的就握着姚冰的手，像是遇到多年失散的老朋友。当他听姚冰说自己是二十多年前从大陆来的工科留学生，目前是一家科技公司的主管时，兴致就更高了。他说自己开了两家成功的上市公司，赚了多少多少钱。又说在大陆认识许多中央领导；甚至叶帅的儿子都是他的哥们。说得姚冰一愣一愣的。他还说自己曾在台湾是有名的歌王，连邓丽君都是他的粉丝。到底谁是谁的粉丝？姚冰默默地在心里计算着他的年龄。他这辈子见过不少会吹牛的，但还真没见过这么会吹的。真的有点吃不消。姚冰暗笑，既然你这么有钱、有名，怎么可能到这种地方来住？牛皮不用戳，自己就破了。

姚冰逃了出来。

等姚冰打发掉晚餐，从外面回来时，艾琳家的整个前后院都停满了车。他数了数，前前后后至少住了七、八个房客，估计前后房子都住满了。

他进了吵吵闹闹的客厅，轻手轻脚地上了楼。此刻他不想再碰到什么人，聊一些无聊的东西。真的陪不起那么多时间。

中间，太太打来电话告诉他，大女儿不知什么原因和男朋友吹了，最近心情很不好。她和姚冰商量要不要飞过去看看她。这么多年，太太为了两个女儿操了很多心。本来她在国内学了一个不错的专业；工作也很称心。然而，跟着姚冰来美国后，一切都要重新开始。艰辛的生活把很多本该有的快乐都散失殆尽了。姚冰经常和太太讨论来美国的对与错。不过，这世上有多少事情可以用黑与白或对与错来衡量？二十几年前开始的出国大潮，把一大批青涩的年轻人一下子推了过来。姚冰就是其中之一。命运常常让人始料未及。有时想想真是荒谬。

姚冰再一次遇见艾琳是在午夜以后。

夜已经深了，房客们陆续都睡觉了，喧闹的房子总算安静下来。这会儿，累了一天的姚冰感到浑身酸痛。他想出去走走。

在楼下，姚冰看见艾琳斜坐在餐桌前，右手握笔在写着什么，左手用劲托着那张疲惫的脸。看见姚冰从楼上下来，她微微一笑算是打了招呼。那双略显浮肿的眼睛里布满了红色的血丝。看样子，她累得连装的力气都没有了。

这么晚了，艾琳还在这里忙碌，姚冰不免有些好奇。他问艾琳，你住在那里？让姚冰没想到的是，他们小俩口并没有一个固定的住所。如果这前后两幢房子中有哪一间没有租出去，他们就住在那一间。

姚冰愣了一下，但没有把这一惊放在脸上。

这时，艾琳说他们还有一家餐厅，此刻她正在整理餐厅的账目。姚冰这才想起艾琳下班后为什么又忙着离开。最后，艾琳还告诉姚冰，她的老公在中国有自己的公司。这会儿他正坐在从上海到旧金山的飞机上往家赶呢。

姚冰瞬间头大了。他细细地算了一下，也就是说，艾琳有一个正式工作，还要忙于一家餐厅，同时还在经营这个爱彼迎(Airbnb)。老公在中国创办了两家公司，常年奔波于中国和美国之间。当然，最让他难以理解的是，他们自己居无定所。这一切只是为了钱？

一个手指同时按下五个跳蚤！

姚冰看着满脸倦容的艾琳，从心底里油然升起对她深深的同情。这是一种什么样的忙，忙到连一丁点的缝隙都没有留给自己；这又是为了什么样的目的而如此地折磨自己。这该是何等的残酷！

· · ·

这一夜，姚冰睡得很浅。

天刚蒙蒙亮，他就被一阵拖行李箱的声音吵醒了。估计是哪个房客离开。等安静下来想再睡一会儿，楼下厨房的抽油烟机又"轰轰"响了起来。倾刻，煎鸡蛋的香味就窜上了楼。又是哪个早起的房客在做早饭。姚冰从床上坐了起来，揉了揉发涩的眼睛。今天对他自己和公司都是关键的一天。如果再把生意谈砸了，大家就要卷铺盖走人。想到这里，姚冰的心脏使劲地拧了一下。

当他早晨下楼时，被眼前的景像吓着了。餐桌上摆满了各种碎碟烂盏。姚冰仔细回想了一下，昨夜并没有听见任何摔盆子掼碗的声音啊；这到底发生了什么？

餐桌边，一个三十多岁的男人正拿着放大镜聚精会神地研究着摊在桌上的碎片。看到姚冰，他抬起头来做了自我介绍。我叫瑟夫，是艾琳的老公。昨夜我刚从中国回来。其实他没开口，姚冰就猜了个八九不离十。

姚冰说，乍一看，我还以为这里是一个正在破案的侦探呢。

瑟夫笑了笑说，还真的有点像，不过，我老婆说我更像考古专家。瑟夫饶有兴至地告诉姚冰，这些都是他刚从中国带回来的宝贝，是康熙年代出土的文物。他想在美国找行家把它们精美地包装起来，然后，再带回中国送给一些生意上的客户。不过瑟夫又说，我老婆怀疑它们是不是百分之百的真货。

姚冰此刻有些糊涂。自己出国时间已经太久了，搞不清楚目前国内的行情。有这样送礼的吗？

看着满脸都写着疑问的姚冰，瑟夫补充道，这些客户真的很重要；我必须舍得花大价钱。

姚冰死死地盯着眼前的这个男人。他才三十出头，就有着半生沧桑的感觉。万里之遥背回这么一堆"珍品"，只是为了在生意上打通关系。看样子，中国生意场上的十八般武艺，他已经掌握了最重要的那部分。要知道，这是一个在美国体制下教育成长的年轻人。真可谓是入乡随俗。

面对着满桌的"珍贵文物"，姚冰真的不想妄加评论。首先把这种残缺的物品作为礼物送人，好像不是中国人的礼仪，更何况送给那些精明的生意人。看样子，瑟夫对中国文化的了解还远不够完整。虽然姚冰对于古董收藏并不在行，但多多少少还是知道一些这个行当中的猫腻和水份。他清楚地记得，在电视节目《天下收藏》里，主持人王刚挥动着金光闪闪的瓜棱槌，砸碎了多少看似完全逼真的赝品。

当瑟夫又告诉姚冰，这些"珍品"是从上海一条繁华街道上的旅游商品店里淘来的，姚冰心里已经基本上明白了。再仔细看看每一片破损杯盘那簇新的边边角角，姚冰感到悲从中来。这些家伙也太能骗了！他们是用什么样的语言，让这个来自西方的小伙子慷慨地掏出巨款，买下这些惨不忍睹的碎片，还像宝贝一样把它们背回来？他有什么能力来鉴定这些物品是否来自康熙年代？

姚冰心里憋得厉害。这个世界是疯了，还是病了？要想在中国生存下来，需要练就一副常在河边走，尽量不湿鞋的本领。如果能在那里做到近墨者不黑，近朱者不赤，才算修行到家了。瑟夫要学的事情还很多。

吃过早饭，姚冰收拾了所有的随身物品，离开了这里，应该说是逃离了这里。出门时，他长长地舒了一口气。

他当即做了一个大胆的决定——摆脱这家公司，不管今天客户的会开得结果如何。

他再也不想让生活之钟，每日摇摆在贪欲和焦虑之间，更不想在无谓的挣扎中迷失一生。在这一片无法清理的凌乱世界里，有多少人在作，在作自己的生命！包括自己。

飨以平淡快乐的生活，至少应该算是成功的一种吧；让自己和自己达成和解，也应该算是成功的另一种。可是，为什么人人非要"成功"呢？现在，姚冰最不喜欢的就是这个词了。

ONE-NIGHT STAY

~

Bing Yao called Eileen and waited in front of her house. She was still nowhere to be seen after thirty minutes. He wondered how it was that young people today couldn't be punctual, even when doing business. The advertisement on the Internet had hyped the place as having a fresh and beautiful environment, cozy and comfortable rooms, and ample daily supplies; it was supposed to be like coming home. *Damnit!* Bing grumbled. *Can't even get in when returning to my own house?*

He circled Eileen's house, wanting to confirm what he had read.

It was a typical American middle-class neighborhood with single-family houses. Because of the high cost of land in San Francisco, every yard was small and exquisite. On the windowsills and inside the fence, the various carefully arranged flowers were showing off in the mellow and pleasant weather.

Bing noticed Eileen's house didn't have flowers planted in the front yard. Only a few cactuses stood there, and some other plants he couldn't name were biting the dust in the sun due to lack of water. Bing also found out that Eileen had built two identical houses, connecting the front one to the back one with a concrete courtyard. For a moment, he couldn't figure out whether the houses belonged to one family or two.

Another ten minutes passed. Bing became impatient. He figured he should give Eileen a bad review online.

Since the company hadn't been doing well for the last two years, his boss had been watching every penny. Now Bing, who used to be able to stay in a star-rated hotel on earlier business trips, had to spend below sixty dollars a night. Man, what kind of hotel would one be able to get in San Francisco for sixty bucks? Not even if you wanted to sleep on a floor. The only option was to get a shared place on Airbnb, which was trendy all over the world. It let owners rent out their homes through the website. Getting a room in a shared place was cheaper than renting an entire house. It was Bing's only choice, which was like having a few dollars left for dinner; one would have to pick McDonald's over a high-end restaurant.

While Bing was pondering, a red Lexus rushed into the driveway.

"I'm sorry!" Eileen shouted as she opened the car door. "I'm so sorry to have kept you waiting. I couldn't get out of a meeting at work today." The hurried voice, along with the sound of high heels thumping on the ground, came before Bing. Then she explained in a rush that this had never happened before. "You know my service and conduct from the remarks left by the previous guests." She said she was feeling sorry for herself as if Bing was writing his review at this very moment. The remarks each tenant left behind would be crucial for future business. Having a good business would be tied in with getting great reviews.

She had a young, good-looking, yet somewhat decrepit face. Tiny beads of sweat dotted her light makeup. Albeit irritated, Bing had swallowed his discontent when she showed up.

"Tomorrow I'll have someone install an electronic bolt," Eileen said as she opened the door. "I'll tell you the code for the bolt, so you won't have to sit tight and wait for me for so long next time." She apologized once more.

It was a two-story house. The area downstairs was not large. You could see the living room, dining room, and kitchen at a glance. Many kinds of Chinese foods, including the "Lao Gan Ma" spicy sauce, filled the kitchen counter, much the same as what she had advertised. It was easy to tell the guests here were mainly Chinese. A golf bag stood against the wall in one corner of the living room. Bing noticed it, as he was a golf enthusiast. "This set has been in the corner for two years," Eileen said. "We're too busy running around every day to have time for fun and exercise."

Eileen had come to the States from mainland China

with her parents in childhood. Her husband was an American-born Chinese (ABC). Bing realized in the middle of the conversation that Eileen was also from Shanghai; the bond brought them closer instantly. Eileen upgraded Bing's room to a larger one upstairs for the same price. More important for Bing, he didn't have to share the bathroom with other guests, which was the way things had been when he'd come to the States twenty years earlier as a student.

The so-called larger room was only big enough to put a bed, a desk, and a chair. Bing took a casual look around the house. There were four rooms upstairs, plus the one he'd initially booked downstairs, for a total of five rooms. It would be a lively place if she rented every one of rooms out. Bing hadn't had this experience for a long time.

After getting Bing settled, Eileen went into the room next door. When she came out, she had changed out of her work clothes and put on a long dress and heavier makeup. She rushed past Bing's room, went downstairs, shut the door, and drove away, engine rumbling and throttle squealing.

Bing shook his head with a wry grin.

The phone buzzed. It was Sarah, Bing's boss. The last person he wanted to deal with right now. *What the heck!* Bing scolded. However, when he picked up the call, his voice was still affable. Well, what would you do? The years had honed his many abilities.

The boss said this customer meeting was pivotal. "We'll survive if you can repair the relationship this time. You must be well prepared, and very, very thorough!"

Sarah's nagging voice almost faded out of Bing's ear as he put the phone aside. "Sarah, you let me clean up the mess. Why not come yourself?" Bing muttered.

Destiny is difficult to predict.

Bing felt he had gone through purgatory since joining this small company four years ago. He had been doing well at a large company, where he'd led a good-sized team and had been respected at all levels. Everything had been smooth sailing. But he'd had lofty ambitions and had resigned on an impulse. What Bing hadn't known was that he'd embarked on a broken ship, wandering and sinking in a stormy sea. To his regret, he hadn't seen Sarah's character from the beginning. She wasn't a doer but a sophisticated and quintessential kiss-up sort of manager. At first glance, Sarah had looked like a gentle old lady; however, she was a devious schemer, a petty micromanager. Working under her, Bing felt that his hands were tied. Whenever the company had a bad quarter, Sarah always evaded taking the responsibility and shifted the blame to her subordinates. If you weren't careful, she'd pick you as her next scapegoat. *Ugh! It's disgraceful, but you asked for it.*

THERE WAS a burst of laughter outside the door. The self-assured laughter rolled into the house as the door opened and went straight upstairs. Bing frowned, figuring the other guests must have come back.

Bing heard the voices of three ladies. The first lady said

the old white man standing across the street had been staring at her. "Do I look so great?"

The other was the voice of a lady with a strong northeastern Chinese accent. She went on to say, "Hey, you beauty. The dress you're wearing today looks very sexy! Even I wanted to see more of you."

The third lady said to the first lady, "He looked at you once and then kept staring at me." With that, the three ladies roared together.

Bing was revising the presentation for the customer meeting tomorrow. The noise disrupted his train of thought in an instant. He wanted to slam the door but felt it wasn't right. As soon as his left hand swung the door hard, his right hand caught it. He then shut it gently, knowing he must control himself. When he'd first come to the company, he had been complacent and full of self-admiration. But after a few rounds with Sarah, he'd realized he must endure everything. It was the best all-around strategy. Honor or disgrace, career ups or downs were merely outward symbols. Keeping the job was most important. Both girls were still in college.

The day was getting late. Bing, who had been occupied on the computer, was hungry. The last meal he'd eaten was on the plane. He'd purchased a small piece of cold sandwich. Even water was not free. No doubt it had been the cheapest flight, another one of the new rules set by Sarah. Recalling that he used to fly business class at the big company, Bing couldn't help feeling an unspeakable loss.

Bing went out for dinner and met a couple at the

doorstep who should be Taiwanese, listening to their accent. The man was tall and fat with a beer belly; his grayish hair was a little greasy. The lady looked old yet still spoke with a babyish voice. Without saying a word, the man grasped Bing's hand like he was a long-lost old friend. He became more animated after Bing said he had come to the States from mainland China over twenty years earlier as an engineering student and was now an executive at a technology company. The man said he had two listed companies and made a lot of money, and he knew many central government leaders on the mainland; even General Ye's son was his best friend. Bing was stunned. The man also said he was a famous singer in Taiwan, and Teresa Teng was his fan. Who was the fan of whom? Bing was figuring his age. He had seen a lot of boasting in his life, yet he had never met someone who bragged so extravagantly. It was too much for him.

Bing chuckled. "Why did you come to this place if you were so rich and famous?" The cowhide broke without being poked.

He got away.

BY THE TIME Bing returned from dinner, Eileen's entire front yard and courtyard were flooded with cars. He tallied them; there must be no fewer than seven or eight lodgers tonight, which would fill up both the front and back houses.

He went through the noisy living room and crept up to his room upstairs, having no desire to meet anyone right now, as he couldn't bear to spend so much time on senseless chatter.

In the middle, his wife called to tell him that the eldest daughter had broken up with her boyfriend and was in an awful mood. She asked if they should fly there to see her. All these years, the wife had been exhausting her energy caring for their two daughters. His wife had pursued a good major; her job was also gratifying. However, everything had to start afresh after she'd come to the States with Bing. The hardship had dispersed many of pleasures they were supposed to have had. Bing and his wife often discussed whether it was right or wrong to immigrate. But, how many things in this world could be measured by black and white or right and wrong? The mega tide of going abroad, which had started over two decades ago, had brought millions of sentimental young people to America. Bing was among them. Changes in fate were often sudden. It was absurd to think about it sometimes.

It was after midnight when Bing saw Eileen again.

The guests all went to bed one after another, and the noisy house was quiet at last. Bing felt sore after a tiring day. He wanted to go for a walk.

Downstairs, Bing saw Eileen leaning over the dining table, writing something with her right hand while her left hand underpinned her weary face. Seeing Bing come down, she greeted him with a smile. Her swollen eyes were bloodshot. She looked so worn out that she had no strength left even to pretend.

Bing wondered why Eileen was still busy here at this time of the night. He asked, "Where do you live?"

To his surprise, the young couple had no permanent place for themselves. They'd sleep in any room in the two houses that wasn't booked.

Bing froze for a moment, yet he didn't show his amazement.

At that point, Eileen told him they also had a restaurant, and she was doing its bookkeeping, which reminded Bing of the way she'd rushed out after work. At last, Eileen told Bing that her husband had companies in China and was sitting on a plane from Shanghai to San Francisco right now, in transit home.

Bing was getting a headache counting the number of things they were juggling. Eileen had a day job but was also managing a restaurant while taking care of this Airbnb business. Her husband was running two start-ups in China, traveling between China and the States. The hardest thing to understand was how they had no fixed place to wind down. Was it all about money?

It's like trying to use one finger to squeeze five fleas!

Facing the exhausted Eileen, Bing was sympathetic to her from the bottom of his heart. *What kind of burden is this? They're too busy to leave even a little breathing space for themselves. How cruel it is to abuse yourself for a particular goal!*

. . .

He didn't sleep well.

The noise of someone towing luggage awoke him at dawn. Maybe a guest was leaving, he thought. He wanted to go back to sleep, but the loud whir of the range hood in the kitchen downstairs started up. The scent of fried egg soon permeated the upstairs. Some early-rising guests were making breakfast. Bing sat up in bed and rubbed his astringent eyes. It was a crucial day for him and the company. If the business talks failed again, everyone would have to pack up and leave. At the thought of this, Bing felt a pinching pain in his chest.

When he came downstairs, he was frightened by what he saw. The dining table was covered with broken dishes. He hadn't heard falling bowls and plates last night; so what had happened?

At the table, a man in his thirties was studying the debris with a magnifying glass. Seeing Bing, he raised his head and introduced himself. "I'm Joseph, Eileen's husband. I came back from China last night." Bing had guessed who he was without his introduction.

"At first glance, I thought a detective was working on a case," Bing said.

Joseph grinned. "It was like that, but my wife said I'm more of an archeologist." He told Bing with great enthusiasm that these were the treasures he had just brought back from China. It was a precious collection of cultural relics unearthed from the Emperor Kangxi era. He wanted to find experts in the States to wrap them up nicely, then bring back to China, where he'd present them to some of his business partners as gifts. However, Joseph added, his wife doubted whether they were one hundred percent genuine.

Bing was dazed for a minute. He had been abroad for a long time and wasn't sure about the current business culture in China. Was this an appropriate gift?

Looking at Bing, whose face was loaded with questions, Joseph added that these customers were indispensable; he must spend a fortune.

Bing gazed at the man before him. He was only in his early thirties but appeared to have endured the vicissitudes of half a life. To develop connections in business, he'd brought back such a heap of "treasures" from thousands of miles away. It looked as if he had mastered the most important part of the eighteen "martial arts" in Chinese business, especially knowing he was a young man brought up and educated under the American system. As the idiom goes, when in Rome, do as the Romans do.

Bing did not comment on the table full of "precious artifacts." First, it wasn't the etiquette of the Chinese people to give these disfigured items as gifts, let alone the custom of those shrewd businessmen. Joseph's knowledge of Chinese culture was far from complete. Although Bing was not an expert on antiques, he knew about a few tricks and forgeries in the industry. Bing remembered that on the TV show *The World Collection*, the host, Mr. Wang, wielded a golden hammer, smashing many fakes that looked utterly authentic.

When Joseph told Bing he'd found these "treasures" in a tourist store on a bustling street in Shanghai, Bing's worries were affirmed. After inspecting the crisp edges of the broken cups and plates, Bing couldn't resist feeling sad. No doubt these guys had skillfully beguiled Joseph. What kind of language had they used to get this young man from the West to pay a huge amount of cash for these horrible fragments and carry them back like babies? Was he qualified to appraise the treasures from the Kangxi era?

Bing's heart tightened. Was the world insane or sick? To survive in China, you'd try not to wet your shoes when working along the riverside. If you could defy the common saying, one takes on the color of one's company, then you'd reached an expert level. Joseph had a long way to go.

BING PACKED his belongings after breakfast and breathed a sigh of relief when he went out. No, he fled from that house.

He made a bold decision—to extricate himself from the company, regardless of the outcome of today's meeting.

He never again wanted the pendulum of life to sway daily between greed and anxiety, nor did he want to lose his life in the meaningless struggle. In this chaotic and tainted world, how many people were agonizing over their own lives, including himself?

Enjoying a plain and joyful life ought to be regarded as a success; reconciliation with yourself ought to be another. But for what reason does everybody need to "succeed"? The word Bing disliked most at this point.

小祖宗

官迈尔斯的警车停在雅芳家门前已有一个多小时了。

贝蒂离家出走也有三天两夜了。

整个家翻了天。雅芳和老公以及二个女儿都请了假,全家发疯似地四处寻找。邻居和朋友们也来帮忙,他们利用各种社交网络正各处问询。

雅芳此刻后悔极了。如果当初自己坚持一下,拒绝弟弟的女儿贝蒂来美国上学,也就不会有今天这么多的麻烦事了。

警官迈尔斯手里拿着笔和本子,仔细记录着雅芳提供的每一个细节,甚至用不用香水,戴什么样的手饰都详细地问到了。最后,迈尔斯说,贝蒂所有的信息都会记录在案。我们在各个巡逻点的警官会加强注意,有消息我们会及时通知你们。他停顿了一下又说,在美国,每年约有五十万小孩失踪。不是每一个人都能找回来的。要看你们的运气了。说完，他颇为沉重地抿了一下嘴。

雅芳的弟弟和弟媳已经到达北京机场。他们订了下午的飞机赶往这边。这两天，雅芳的手机被他们打暴了。尤其是弟媳，恨不得不让雅芳挂电话。虽然她没有破口大骂，但很多难听话都倾泻了过来。雅芳能理解她的焦虑；可是自己的苦衷她知道吗？她有多了解自己的女儿？

雅芳还清楚地记得三年前全家把贝蒂从机场接回家的那一天。当时，贝蒂坐的上海飞往洛杉矶的飞机已经降落两个小时了，可她还没有露面。雅芳焦急地给弟弟打电话。弟弟说，昨天在上海机场，他们把女儿送到安检口，看着她从那里消失的。弟弟还查询了贝蒂在北京机场的登机记录，确认她上了那趟飞机。

正当大家万分焦急的时候，贝蒂戴着耳机，怡然自得、慢慢悠悠地从出口走了出来。原来，她嫌飞机上的饭不好吃，下了飞机后在机场里面挑个餐厅吃饭去了。

取行李时，贝蒂站在一边。当她的两只超大的行李箱从传送带上缓缓而来的时候，她朝雅芳看了一眼，然后用手指了指。雅芳的老公和两个女儿连忙跑过去把它们拖了下来。雅芳倒吸了一口气，心想，来了个小祖宗。

雅芳只有一个弟弟。两人的关系不能说有多好。来自中国北方的父母多少有些重男轻女。从小在家中，几乎所有家务活都是雅芳做。衣服基本上也是弟弟穿新的，而雅芳只能捡妈妈穿旧的。有一次，雅芳实在气不过，斗胆向父母抗议：为什么家中的事弟弟不能分担？爸爸有些看不过去，把饭后洗碗的活儿给了弟弟。谁知从那以后，弟弟每次吃过饭都会躲在洗手间里。妈妈看着满桌的脏碗筷，瞪起眼睛就骂雅芳。结果洗碗的事就又归了雅芳。

雅芳出国没几年，弟弟就下岗了。姐弟俩巨大的反差，让雅芳觉得欠了弟弟很多。不仅平时寄钱给父母，时不时还要补贴弟弟一家。贝蒂的很多衣服，都是雅芳这个姑姑买的。每次回国大包小包地送，苹果手机、平板电脑一样都不缺。连平时不管事的老公，都颇有意见。

雅芳的手机响了。电话来自市警察分局的一个华人女警官。听到同胞的声音，雅芳顿时感到一阵慰藉。女警官用中文告诉她，贝蒂的失踪已经正式立案，她是专门分派来管这个案子的。如果有什么新的进展，让雅芳直接和她联系。

这三天，雅芳基本上没合眼，也没吃什么东西。她感到极度的疲惫。——一种从来都没有过的累。她靠在沙发上，闭上了眼睛。

贝蒂来美国时，只有十三岁，是来上初中的。

开始，雅芳并不同意弟弟和弟媳把女儿送到美国来上学，理由是年龄太小，各方面都不太成熟。她认为孩子应该在父母的身边成长。她不能想象自己的女儿在这个年龄离开家。然而雅芳最终还是没能拧过他们。他们把道理讲得一套一套的：什么不想错过学语言的最佳年龄，什么不想让聪明过人的女儿毁在死板的中国教育体制下，等等。让雅芳找不出足够的理由来拒绝。

那天，把贝蒂从机场接到家的情景还历历在目。

两只超大的行李箱被打开了。一个箱子里装满了各种款式的名牌衣服，其中很多是雅芳以前买的，还有各类女孩子的饰品、玩具。另一个箱子里几乎全是五颜六色、令人弦目的零食和小吃:"三只松鼠"的坚果大礼包;包装精美的"百草味"蜜饯话梅;"良品铺子"的甜辣味小鱼干;"华味享","来伊份"——简直可以开一家零食专卖店。最后,贝蒂从箱角拿出一条丝巾扔给雅芳说,这是我妈送你的。

雅芳还记得在前一阵子和弟弟来来回回的电话中,弟弟曾问过雅芳喜欢什么样的礼物,好让弟媳帮着挑选。从电话中,雅芳清晰地听见弟媳没好气的声音,烦死了!我怎么知道给她买什么?当时,雅芳心里就不太舒服。这条丝巾应该就是弟弟当时说起的礼物。

贝蒂合上两个塞得满满的箱子,让雅芳老公把它们抬到楼上那间给她准备的房间去。临上楼还丢下一句话,我妈让你明天给我买一台电脑,要名牌的。说完就"噔噔"地上楼了,留下满脸惊愕的全家。

从机场见面到现在,贝蒂没喊过雅芳一声姑姑。

雅芳的手机又响了。是大女儿打来的。她和妹妹正在为寻找贝蒂四处奔波。她们去贝蒂学校的同学、朋友那里挨个问过,至今没有发现什么线索。大女儿还有一年高中就毕业了,上个月刚考完SAT。二女儿正在上初中。让雅芳感到欣慰的是两个女儿都心地善良,乐于助人。对待贝蒂,她们表现得宽容、友善,让雅芳自叹不如。这几年,雅芳因把太多的精力花在贝蒂身上,深深地觉得对不起两个女儿。尤其是老公,经常出差,回到家后也得不到放松。

贝蒂刚来的头几个月,是雅芳最抓狂的。她的英文不好,上课听不懂;在学校吃不惯西餐;没有朋友。每天晚上，雅芳都要抽出时间辅导她的功课，而常常看到的是一张兴味索然的脸。两个女儿经常试着用英文和她聊天，努力帮她提高英语会话水平。可是，她们的兴趣相差太远了，经常话不投机。

贝蒂最感兴趣的就是看韩剧，几乎知道所有韩国的男明星。每当她艳羡地谈起李敏镐、金秀贤和郑智薰时，脸上常露出无限陶醉的表情，让雅芳的两个女儿看得云里雾里的。而大多数时间里，她只待在自己的房间里。每天下楼吃饭时，要么戴着耳机听音乐，要么低头看手机，还经常旁若无人地大声和国内朋友用微信聊天。有时雅芳想和她说几句话，看着她那不屑一顾的表情，又咽了回去。

一次，雅芳下班晚了。回家后烘了冷冻彼萨，拌了沙拉。贝蒂从楼上下来吃饭，看到桌上的晚餐不对自己的胃口，一句话没说，扭头就回楼上了，进了房间"嘭"一声关上了门。雅芳老公看不下去了，忽地站了起来。雅芳赶紧拉了拉他的袖子小声说，算了，不是自己的孩子，说什么话，做什么事都要谨慎些。

老公满脸愠色，说，都是你惯的。

雅芳无耐地摇了摇头，叹了口气说，你还看不出来？她这种性格能这么快就形成吗？

一个星期一的中午，雅芳正在公司开会。中间接到贝蒂从学校打来的电话。一串怒不可遏的话语从电话中嚷了过来，声音之大连旁边的同事都能听见。雅芳赶紧退到了走廊。

贝蒂用苛责的语气说，你为什么不给我带午餐？

雅芳说，你们学校每天不是都提供午餐吗？

没有，今天没有。贝蒂的声音简直在吼。

雅芳竭力控制住自己的声调说，你没有告诉我呀？

学校也没有发通知。

有，有通知。贝蒂的声音仍然理直气壮。

这次雅芳提高了嗓门，你把通知给我了吗？

晚上，雅芳下班回家才发现学校上个星期五就发了通知，只是贝蒂留在书包里自己忘了拿出来。

这次雅芳真的生气了。她一字一句地告诉贝蒂，要学会尊重，学会担当，学会感恩！她又说了很多，每一句话都谨慎选择自己的用词。这次，贝蒂若有所思地抬起了眼睛。

贝蒂长期不在父母身边。雅芳在合理的情况下还是尽量满足她的要求。周末会抽空包些饺子、包子。贝蒂说喜欢吃粽子，雅芳也会不等到端午节就给她包一些。雅芳想，孩子还小，慢慢地总会被感动的。

平时，雅芳在工作忙的时候，常常买些大包装的西餐，然后分装成小份冻在冰箱里。下班后，把这些冰冻的食物放在烘箱或微波炉里热一下，配一些蔬菜沙拉，一顿饭就解决了。

一次，小女儿看见贝蒂吃饺子，也想吃几个。谁知贝蒂把眼睛一瞪，撇了撇嘴说，这是我的饺子，是你妈给我包的。她把这两个"我"字都加了重音。

听到这些话，平时很不再意的小女儿，两眼顿时汪出了泪水。

雅芳感觉有些不太对头，和蔼地对贝蒂说，好东西要大家一起分享。一家人住在一起更要彼此关爱。

话还没落音，贝蒂气咻咻地猛地站了起来，把几乎满盘的饺子一下倒进了垃圾桶。

雅芳难以想像，这个孩子是在怎样的环境中长大的。她毫不珍惜别人为她付出的一切。更让人担忧的是她对自己行为的对与错浑然无觉。雅芳不想把这些事情都归咎于她。在浑水中长大的孩子，你能让她至清至纯吗？

前一段时间，雅芳给三个孩子分配了一些简单的家务活。没过两天，弟媳的电话就打过来了。她用讥讽的语调说，我们家贝蒂从小到大从来没让她做过家务。她的任务就是学习。百分之百的时间都要用在学习上。她不是去你那里做小保姆的！

雅芳能和弟媳说什么呢？吵架吗？每次弟媳打电话过来，一句废话都没有，单刀直入，就是要给贝蒂吃什么，穿什么，用什么。让人感觉雅芳倒像是贝蒂的贴身老保姆。许多责备和讥讽的弦外之音让雅芳无法置信。雅芳不需要弟弟、弟媳对自己感激涕零，但是，他们也不能对别人的付出视若无睹吧。

又是半天过去了，还是没有任何消息。雅芳这两天一直在反躬自省，她没有觉得自己做错了什么。如果贝蒂的很多行为再不加以纠正，她就要被毁掉了。

有一段时间，家里经常收到贝蒂从网上订购的各种快递包裹。后来才知道，她为了能在朋友和同学的生日聚会中送得出手，阔卓大方地买了高档化妆品、手饰和名牌衣服。慢慢地她的零花钱就不够用了。弟弟家的生活并没有那么优渥，可是贝蒂在外面举手投足都秀出富二代的范儿。雅芳很耐心地告诉她，虽然我们的生活并不拮据，可我们也不能像这样花钱。

每次听到类似的话，不等雅芳说完，贝蒂都会不屑地扭头就走。可是，不管她爱听不听，雅芳还是要说。这次看她没有要挪步的意思，雅芳把语调放得更平静、更缓和。她说，如果一个人的内心不够强大和自信，往往就需要用外在的显摆来提高自己的气场，从中获得别人对你的尊敬。其实这是一种自卑的表现。雅芳停顿了一下，她不知道贝蒂能否理解这些话。贝蒂眼睛斜睨着，没有说话。雅芳暗自高兴，以为这次她听进去了，想继续往下说。

我爸每月给的钱都被你们家吞掉了！突然，贝蒂嘴里没头没脑蹦出这么一句。说完，还"嗤"了声。

贝蒂的话完全不挨边搭界。看着眼前这个乖戾的孩子，雅芳真的难以容忍下去了。雅芳想告诉她，你爸给我的钱连供你吃饭都不够。她还想说，你给我们家带来的这种肆虐之苦，就是给我们再多的钱，我们也不想承受。

雅芳没有说，也不能说。再怎么说她还是个孩子。雅芳感到做为她的姑姑，自己有责任教育她，可是又那么无能为力。

有很多次，她想向弟弟坦诚相告，你们的女儿不能再这样下去了。可是她何尝不知道，弟弟在家完全做不了主。自从他下岗后，一直都没有一个正式的工作。在弟媳眼里，他就是个吃软饭的人。在这种反差巨大的家庭里，又有这么强势的老婆，雅芳说什么都只能引起他们的争吵，甚至是家庭的撕裂。此刻的雅芳，进退维谷，伤透了脑筋。

雅芳的头痛得像要裂开似的。她真想睡上一会儿，那怕是一小会儿。如果贝蒂再找不到，真不敢想象那将是什么样的后果。明天弟弟和弟媳就要到了。她要准备好迎接一场风暴。

雅芳不想推诿责任，毕竟贝蒂是从这里出走的。但是把一切责任都归咎于自己，也太不公平了。此刻，她感到无限悲哀，——为贝蒂，也为自己。

雅芳努力地回忆最近发生的事情。

半年前，雅芳接到贝蒂学校辅导员打来的电话，说贝蒂班上的同学在她身上闻到了酒味，让雅芳确认一下。还说，这是一个严肃的事情。美国法律规定，二十一岁以下的人不能买酒或饮酒。如果继续下去，贝蒂将被学校开除。

晚上，雅芳把学校辅导员的话，逐字逐句地告诉了贝蒂，并告诉她问题的严重性。贝蒂坚决否认，并说，是那帮恨她的同学在造谣。雅芳这次选择相信她。她想，一个不到十六岁的小女孩，商店也不会卖酒给她啊。自己还记得刚到美国没多久，为一次朋友聚会去买酒。当时店员一定要她出示驾驶执照，好确定是否已满二十一岁，可她那时已经三十了。

学校打过电话没几天，雅芳自己也隐隐约约闻到贝蒂身上的酒味。问题没那么简单！雅芳蓦然想起家里贮藏多年的那瓶从国内带来的茅台酒。果然，一直放在厨房食品柜里的那瓶酒不见了。她先挨个问了家里的其他人。他们都说没有拿。这下雅芳彻底明白了。她找到了藏在楼上贝蒂房间里的那瓶只剩下一半的酒瓶，还意外地发现了两瓶其他的酒。

面对眼前的证物，贝蒂很不以为然。她轻描淡写地说，不就是喝了点酒吗？有什么了不起的。在我五岁的时候，我爸就用筷子沾白酒让我舔了。这值得大惊小怪吗？说完，抬着头绝决地加了一句，以后少管我的闲事！

雅芳看着那张不明是非、任性骄纵的脸，一股寒气直渗到心底。她可以理解这个年龄孩子的叛逆；也可以容忍孩子成长时期的少不更事；然而，她不能理解也不能容忍那种从骨子里溢出来的唯我独尊和薄情寡义。

雅芳思忖再三，还是决定给弟媳打电话。她没有把贝蒂俯拾即是的毛病通通讲出来；但是，她告诉了弟媳贝蒂的一些问题，一些可能在他们看来是小毛病，而最终会酿成大问题的问题。

这一通电话虽然没有吵架，但是，过后却加深了贝蒂和整个家庭的隔阂。

从这以后，贝蒂经常隔三差五的晚回来，而且拒绝告诉理由。害得雅芳下班后还要赶到学校，或是打电话去她的同学那里四处寻问。有时她会在同学家过夜，也不愿意告诉同学的姓名和地址，让雅芳全家倍感担心。

有一天早晨，贝蒂从同学家过夜回来，雅芳彻底怒了。她瞪着眼睛，用自己都不敢相信的声音，言之凿凿地警告贝蒂，如果再有一次这样的行为，就立即将她送回国。

这次，贝蒂真的被震慑住了。她嘴唇微微翕动了几下，什么话也没说出来。

自从这次雅芳发火之后，家里总算安静了一段时间。直到有一天，雅芳打扫贝蒂的房间时，在她的枕头下发现了白粉和避孕工具。这个发现彻底打破了雅芳的底线。

震惊、恐惧和忧虑！雅芳此刻陷入绝望之中。

让一个没有成熟直觉和顿悟的孩子，过早地离开自己父母，放入美国这个凌乱的社会，是一件多么危险和不靠谱的事情。

雅芳一直想竭尽所能帮助贝蒂，可是这一个接着一个的失望让她深信，自己面对的是没有渗透一点希望的绝望。

这次,她下定决心让贝蒂回国。不能让她毁在这里。

天慢慢地暗了下来。还是一点消息都没有。

雅芳想,如果当时退而求次,睁一只眼闭一只眼,是不是就不会发生这次的事情。可是现在想什么都已于事无补了。她让老公和两个女儿都去睡一会。大家都熬在这里没有任何意义。该做的都已经做了。现在只能在心里千乞万求:小祖宗,你这次千万别出事!

大约在后半夜,雅芳迷迷糊糊地听到门铃声。她迅速冲过去开门。

门廊的灯光下,一个头发染成彩色的白人男孩,正扶着喝得醉如烂泥的贝蒂。男孩的鼻子上钉着二个银色的圆环格外醒目。他没有和雅芳说话,把歪歪倒倒的贝蒂放下后,扭头就走了。雅芳大大地松了一口气。这几天雅芳设想过各种可能的结果,这无疑是最好的一个。她一把搂住贝蒂,眼泪"刷"地落了下来。

明天,贝蒂的爸爸妈妈就要到了。能把她完整地交给他们是雅芳这三天时刻都在祈祷的景象。

她要郑重地告诉他们,贝蒂真的需要他们。孩子需要父母!在这个世界上,没有哪一种缺失比这种缺失更可怕了!!

A LITTLE DEVIL

Officer Myers's squad car had been parked in front of Avon's house for more than an hour.

It had been three days and two nights since Betty had run away from home.

The whole house had been turned upside down. Avon, her husband, and their two daughters had all taken time off, and the family had frantically searched everywhere. Neighbors and friends also came to help, and they made inquiries using various social networks.

Avon was full of regret now. *Had I refused to allow my brother's daughter to come to America for her schooling and stay with us, there wouldn't have been so many troubles today.*

With a pen and a notebook in his hands, Officer Myers kept a careful record of every detail Avon provided, even asking what kind of perfume Betty used and what bracelets she wore. At last, Officer Myers said he had recorded all of Betty's information. Their officers would be on the lookout at each patrol point, and they'd keep the family posted. He paused and added that in the United States, about half a million children go missing every year. Not every person can be found. It depended on your luck. With that, his lips pressed hard together.

Avon's brother and sister-in-law had arrived at the Beijing airport and booked an afternoon flight to get here. They'd bombarded Avon's mobile phone in the last three days. Her sister-in-law wouldn't let Avon hang up. Although there had been no swearing, a lot of offensive words had poured over. Avon could understand her anxiety; *But does she know my struggles? How much did she know about her daughter?*

Avon remembered that night three years ago when the family had taken Betty home from the airport. Two hours after her flight from Shanghai to Los Angeles had landed, Betty hadn't shown up. Avon had been worried and had called her brother, who'd said they'd sent their daughter to the security checkpoint yesterday and watched her disappear. Her brother had checked Betty's boarding record at Beijing airport and confirmed she had boarded the plane.

While everyone was on edge, Betty, wearing headphones, strolled out of the exit at ease with herself. It turned out she hadn't cared for the food served on the plane and had picked a restaurant to eat at inside the terminal.

Betty stood by while waiting for her luggage. She glanced at Avon as two oversized suitcases came from the conveyor belt, then pointed at them with her finger. Avon's husband and two daughters had hurried to drag them down. Avon had taken a deep breath and thought to herself, *Here comes a little devil.*

Avon had only one brother. The relationship between the two could not be portrayed as good. Parents from northern China were more men-centric. At home, Avon had had to do almost all the housework since childhood. While her brother wore new clothes, Avon only had her mom's secondhand castoffs. On one occasion, Avon had been so furious she'd dared to protest against her parents. Why couldn't her brother share the chores? Dad had gotten involved and given the dishwashing task to her brother. After that, her brother would hide in the bathroom each time he finished eating. Looking at the messy dishes and chopsticks all over the table, their mother had glared at Avon and scolded her. The dishwashing job had gone back to Avon.

A few years after Avon went abroad, her younger brother got laid off. The contrast between the siblings made Avon feel sorry for her brother. Not only did she often send cash to her parents, but she also subsidized her brother's family from time to time. Many of Betty's clothes were bought by Avon. Every time she returned to China, she brought them many presents, including iPhones and tablets. Even her husband, who was rather hands-off when it came to family affairs, had issues with it.

Avon's phone rang. It was a Chinese female officer in the city's police division. Avon felt a sense of comfort at hearing the voices of her compatriots. The officer told Avon in Chinese that Betty's missing persons case had been filed and she had been assigned to handle it. Avon could contact her directly if there were any new developments.

Avon hadn't slept or eaten much over the last three days. Depleted as never before, she leaned back on the couch and closed her eyes.

When Betty had come to America, she was only thirteen years old and attending middle school.

At first, Avon hadn't agreed with her brother and his wife's decision to send their daughter to the States, believing she was too young to be mature. Avon also believed children should grow up around their parents. It was hard to imagine her little girls leaving home at that age. But, Avon had failed to persuade them. They were brimming with justifications: Betty shouldn't miss the best time to learn a new language, and they didn't want China's rigid educational system to ruin a brilliant girl. Avon couldn't find enough reasons to turn them down.

The scene from the day they'd brought Betty home from the airport was still vivid in her mind.

The two oversized suitcases were opened. One was filled with designer clothes, many of which Avon had bought for Betty before, and all kinds of girls' trimmings and toys. The other one was loaded with colorful snacks. There were "Three Squirrels" assorted nuts in a big gift box; well-packaged "Herbal Flavor" candied plum; "Good Taste Shop" sweet and spicy dried fish. There were also snacks by "Delicious Chinese" and "Laini Powder"—enough to open

A Little Devil

a snack shop. At last, Betty took out a silk scarf from the corner of one suitcase and tossed it to Avon, saying, "My mother gave this to you."

Avon had recalled the back-and-forth phone calls with her brother a while ago. He'd asked her what present she'd like to have so her sister-in-law could help pick it out. On the phone, Avon heard her sister-in-law's upset voice. "Gosh! How do I know what to buy for her?" It made Avon feel awkward. This silk scarf must be the present her brother had suggested.

Betty closed the two heavy suitcases and asked Avon's husband to carry them upstairs to the room prepared for her. On the way up, she said, "My mom asked you to buy me a computer tomorrow. I want a famous brand." Then she stomped into her room, leaving the whole family in astonishment.

Betty hadn't called Avon "Auntie" since they'd met at the airport.

AVON'S PHONE RANG AGAIN. It was her elder daughter. She and her sister were running around looking for Betty. They had asked Betty's friends and the students at her school one by one and had found no clues. The elder daughter would graduate from high school in one year and had taken the SAT last month. The second daughter was in middle school. Avon was grateful that both daughters were kindhearted and accommodating. When dealing with Betty, they showed tolerance and friendliness, making Avon feel inferior. Having been spending too much energy on Betty in recent years, Avon was sorry for her daughters, and especially her husband, who traveled often yet couldn't relax when he came home.

Avon had freaked out the most during Betty's first few months here. Her English wasn't sufficient to understand her classes; she couldn't get used to Western foods in school; and she had no friends. Every night, Avon set aside time to help her with homework but was often met by an indifferent look on Betty's face. The two daughters tried to talk with her in English to develop her conversational skills. However, their interests were so far apart that there was little for them to discuss.

Betty was most intrigued by watching Korean dramas and knew almost all the Korean male stars. When she was adoring Lee Min-ho, Kim Soo-hyun, and Jung Ji-hoon, her face showed an infinite intoxication, leaving Avon's two daughters befogged. She spent most of her time in her room. When she came downstairs at mealtimes, she'd either listen to music with her headphones on or look down at her cell phone, often talking loudly with her friends in China on WeChat as if there was nobody in the room. Sometimes Avon wanted to speak to her but swallowed her words after seeing her dismissive look.

Once, Avon left work late. She baked a frozen pizza and made a salad after returning home. Betty came to eat and saw the dinner on the table wasn't to her taste. Without saying a word, she went back upstairs, entered her room, and slammed the door with a bang. Avon's husband couldn't hold back any longer and popped up from his chair. Avon pulled him by the sleeve and whispered, "Stop it. She's not your kid. Be careful what you say and do."

Her husband looked morose and said, "You spoiled her."

Avon shook her head and sighed. "Don't you see? Could her character have been shaped so fast?"

One Monday at noon, Avon was in a meeting at her company. In the middle of it, Betty called from school. A flood of angry words poured out of her, her voice so loud that Avon's colleagues overheard. Avon ran out to the hallway.

Betty scolded, "Why didn't you bring me lunch?"

"Doesn't your school provide lunch every day?" Avon asked.

"No, not today," Betty thundered.

Avon tried her best to control her voice. "Did you tell me? The school didn't send me a notice."

"Yes, there was a notice," Betty argued.

Avon raised her voice this time. "Did you give me the notice?"

That evening, Avon came home from work only to find that the school had sent a notice last Friday, but Betty had left it in her backpack and neglected to take it out.

Avon was mad. She told Betty she should learn how to respect, to be tolerant, and to be grateful! She said a lot more, picking her words with care. Betty thoughtfully raised her eyebrows this time.

Betty had been away from her parents for several years.

Avon tried her best to satisfy her needs under reasonable circumstances. She'd make dumplings and buns on the weekends. Hearing that Betty loved zongzi, Avon would make some for her outside of the Dragon Boat festival. Avon thought, *The child is still young; she'll be moved over time.*

During times when she was busy at work, Avon would often buy large packages of Western food and split them up to stuff the fridge. After work, she'd heat the frozen food in the oven or the microwave, add a salad, and then dinner would be ready.

Once, her younger daughter saw Betty eating dumplings and also wanted to have some. Betty glared and curled her lips. "These are my dumplings. Your mom made them for *me*." She stressed the word *me*.

The younger daughter, who was most easygoing, burst into tears.

Avon felt Betty was being unreasonable and kindly told her they needed to share good things at home. The family should care for each other when living together.

Before she could finish speaking, Betty rose in outrage and poured almost a full plate of dumplings into the trash can.

Avon couldn't imagine the environment in which she had grown up. She didn't appreciate what others did for her. More troubling, she was oblivious to the right and wrong of her actions. Avon didn't want to point the finger at her. Could you take a child who had grown up in muddy water and make her pure and polished?

Some time ago, Avon had assigned the three children

simple chores. Within two days, her sister-in-law had called. "In our family, we never asked Betty to do chores at home," she said in a mocking tone. "Her task is to learn. She must spend one hundred percent of her time studying. Betty didn't go to your place to be your little maid."

What could Avon say to her sister-in-law? She didn't want to argue with her. Whenever her sister-in-law called, there was not a single unnecessary word. It was straight to the point and all about Betty—what Betty should eat, wear and do. It made Avon seem like Betty's old nanny. Many reproachful and sarcastic overtones left Avon in disbelief. She hadn't expected them to appreciate her, but they shouldn't turn a blind eye to the efforts of others either.

ANOTHER HALF DAY PASSED. Still no news. Avon had been reflecting on herself for the past three days, and she didn't feel she had done anything wrong. Betty would be ruined if she didn't correct many of her behaviors.

For a period, Avon's family often received various packages that Betty had ordered online. Only later did Avon find out that Betty had generously bought top-of-the-line cosmetics, rings and bracelets, and designer clothes as birthday presents for her friends and classmates. Before long, her pocket money had run out. Although Avon's brother's family wasn't affluent, Betty showed off her rich second-generation style by acting like it. Avon told her patiently, "While we weren't living on a strict budget, we shouldn't spend money like that."

Every time Betty heard this, she'd turn her head disdainfully and stalk off before Avon could finish. However, whether she liked it or not, Avon still had to say it. Once, seeing she didn't intend to break away, Avon slowed down further and said calmly that if a person's heart wasn't secure and confident enough, he or she often needed to use external displays to lift his or her aura and gain the respect of others. In fact, this was a sign of inferiority. Avon paused, wondering if Betty could understand. Betty squinted at her and said nothing. Avon was pleased had Betty listened this time and wanted to continue.

"Your family gulped the money my daddy sent!" Betty suddenly blurted out, then snorted.

Betty's words were completely out of bounds. Looking at the grumpy child before her, Avon couldn't stand it anymore. Avon wanted to tell her that her father hadn't given them enough money to feed her, and that, regardless of how much money they got, they'd prefer not to endure the misery Betty had brought to their family.

Avon did not say, nor could she say, those words. Anyway, Betty was still a child. Avon felt that as her aunt, she had the obligation to mold her. But there seemed to be nothing she could do.

Many times, she wanted to tell her brother, "Your daughter can't go on like this." But she knew her brother wasn't the one in charge at home. Since he had been laid off, he hadn't had a formal job. In the eyes of Avon's sister-in-law, her brother was a kept man. In such a family, dominated by a strong wife, anything Avon could say would

A Little Devil

only prompt arguments, or even break up the family. Avon was in a bewildering dilemma at the moment, enough to give her gray hair.

Avon had a splitting headache. She wanted to nap for a minute. The consequences would be unthinkable if Betty couldn't be found soon. Her brother and his wife would arrive tomorrow. She should be prepared for a tempest.

Avon didn't like to pass the buck. In any case, Betty had run away from here. But it'd be unfair to lay all the blame on her. She was dejected at the moment—for Betty and for herself.

Avon struggled to recall recent events.

Six months ago, Avon had gotten a call from a counselor at Betty's school, saying Betty's classmates had smelled alcohol on her and asking Avon to probe. It was a serious matter, said the counselor. US law stipulated that people under the age of twenty-one couldn't buy or drink alcohol. They would expel Betty from school if she continued.

In the evening, Avon told Betty word for word what the school counselor had said and how serious the matter was. Betty disavowed the accusation and said students who hated her had made it up. Avon had chosen to trust her this time. She thought the store wouldn't sell liquor to a young lady under sixteen. She still remembered when, not long after she'd arrived in the States, she had gone to buy wine for a friend's party. The shop clerk had asked her to show her driver's license to check if Avon was over twenty-one when she was already thirty.

Within days of the school's phone call, Avon had detected a faint smell of liquor on Betty. It appeared the problem wasn't that simple. Avon suddenly remembered the bottle of Moutai that had been at home for years. Sure enough, the jar in the pantry had disappeared. First, she asked the rest of the family one by one. All said they hadn't taken it. Now Avon knew all about that. She'd discovered the bottle, half-consumed, hidden in Betty's room upstairs and found two other bottles of alcohol by accident.

Betty was dismissive when confronted with the evidence. "What's the big deal?" she'd said. "I just drank a little alcohol. When I was five years old, my daddy used chopsticks to dip into the white liquor and let me lick it. Is it worth all this fuss?" With that, she added, with her chin up, "Stay out of my business!"

Avon had looked at the unruly, willful, and arrogant face, and a chill seeped straight to the bottom of her heart. She could understand the defiant offspring of this age, and could also tolerate ignorance during the child's growth period; however, she couldn't understand or tolerate the egotism and coldness that overflowed from the girl.

On second thought, Avon decided to call her sister-in-law. She wouldn't tell her all the bad habits Betty had picked up; however, she wanted to tell her about some issues that might seem minor to them but could lead to significant problems later.

Although there had been no quarrel on the phone, the

call had later deepened Betty's estrangement from the family.

Since then, Betty often came home late and refused to explain. After work, Avon had to go to the school or call her classmates to locate her. Sometimes, she would spend a night at a classmate's house and wouldn't tell them the classmate's name and address, leaving Avon's family worried.

On a morning when she'd returned from a sleepover at her classmate's house, Avon was so furious that she glared at Betty and warned her in a voice she couldn't believe herself that if she did this again, she'd send her back to China at once.

This time, she was intimidated. Her lips moved a few times slightly without saying a word.

Avon's outburst brought a period of peaceful time for the family. Until one day, she found white powders and contraceptives under Betty's pillow while cleaning her room. The discovery stunned Avon.

Shock, fear, and anxiety! Avon was in despair.

How perilous and problematic to let a child without mature intuition and insight leave her parents early and place her in the muddled society of America.

Avon had been itching to do everything possible to help Betty, but one disappointment after another had convinced her that the despair she faced was hopeless.

This time, Avon was determined to bring Betty home. She'd not let her be destroyed here.

. . .

It was getting dark. There was still no news.

Perhaps this wouldn't have happened if I had retreated and turned a blind eye, she thought. But it was no use thinking about it now. She asked her husband and two daughters to go to bed. There was no point in everybody waiting up. All that should be done had already been done. She could only pray in her heart, over and over: *Little devil, you must be okay this time.*

About midnight, Avon heard the doorbell in a daze. She rushed to open the door.

Under the porch light, a white boy with dyed hair was holding Betty, who was drunk like a pile of mud. The two silver rings hanging from the boy's nose were striking. He didn't speak to Avon, just put Betty down and turned away. Avon felt a tremendous relief. She thought that of the many possible outcomes, this was the best one. She wrapped an arm around Betty; the tears rolled down.

Betty's parents would arrive tomorrow. Handing over Betty to them in one piece was the scene Avon had been praying for over the past three days.

She wanted to tell them that Betty needed them. *Children need parents!* In this world, there was no loss more terrible than this one!

错位

清晨，天还没亮，卧室墙角上方的声音又出现了。不大不小，刚好听见。"窸窸窣窣"的声音在每次之后都有以秒计的间断。子卉默默地数着，一共八次。

近来，子卉被这种声音折磨得疲惫不堪。声音很蹊跷，从时间到次数都非常固定。第一次是在厨房听见的。那天傍晚天快黑了，她坐在桌边喝茶，头顶上响起了很轻的磨擦声。声音在寂静的屋子里格外清晰。开始她并没在意，也许是风声吧。接下来的几天里，同样的声音在同样的时间里又出现了。她仔细数着：每次都响了八下。

这下让子卉陷入了恐慌。当最后一次声音过后，她再也沉不住气了，抓起电话打到北京。这时老公正在开会。

子卉声音颤抖、颠三倒四地说着这些听起来有些诡异的事情。老公耐着性子听了半天，也没弄清家里到底发生了什么事情。

"我今天这个会很重要，实在没有时间。你去找罗姐。"说完，他挂了电话。

子卉的老公三年前去了北京。他辞掉了在美国干了十几年的不痛不痒的工作后，走得毅然决然。

罗姐是从中国武汉来美国陪儿子读书的，和子卉同住一个小区。自从儿子上初中后，时间就空出来了。两个老公都不在身边的女人很快就聊到了一起。

罗姐说："这很简单，我们俩里应外合。我守在房子外面，等声音一出现，你就发信息给我。"

傍晚，天还没全黑，罗姐已经蹲在了子卉家后院的丁香树丛后面。她目不转睛地盯着厨房的屋顶，屏息啼听，等候子卉发来指令。

不一会儿，罗姐的手机微微地颤了一下。果然，眼前有了动静。影约中，一只硕大的老鼠，从厨房墙角的屋顶上探出头来。罗姐屏住呼吸，瞪大眼睛。第一只应该是领头的。它扭动了几下脑袋，像是在探察周围的情况。几秒钟后，一只接着一只，在淡淡的暮色中鱼贯而出。

罗姐的心跳开始加速。女人都怕老鼠，罗姐也怕。国内的老鼠也就是二、三寸长的小老鼠，这里的洋老鼠个个长得像小猫似的。她一个一个地数着，一共八只。它们浩浩荡荡又消无声息地从屋顶上"哧溜"下来，一眨眼就不见了。

罗姐如实地告诉了子卉。子卉傻眼了。

· · ·

子卉从小就怕三样东西：老鼠，死人和黑暗。她记得，它们经常同时出现在一些电影的场景中。父亲和老公都笑她，死人有什么好怕的，活人才可怕。可是子卉不怕活人。小时候，她可以和最调皮的男孩打架。但是她怕死人，因为她不明白一个好好的人怎么就不动了呢？从小父亲就告诉她，人都要死的，再伟大的人也一样。具体人死后去了哪里，父亲也不知道。没人知道才害怕，这是子卉的结论。

清晨出现在卧室头顶上的声音总算弄清楚了——老鼠，至少八只，住在头顶的阁搂里。一个大家庭，不请自来。

一个电话又打到了北京。

老公急了，说："不就是老鼠吗？这么大个人还能被老鼠吓着？俗话说胆小如鼠。老鼠是生物链的底层。你怕它们干啥？"

理是这个理；可怕就是怕。很少有女人不怕老鼠的。子卉能讲出一串子理由：卑鄙肮脏，长相猥琐，偷偷摸摸。偶然撞上，它们就仓皇逃窜，让人本能地毛骨悚然。

老公说："昼伏夜出的本性是上帝给的，这事不能全怪它们，身不由己呀。"

"去，去。你说得轻松。"

"你和它们井水不犯河水，惹不起躲得起。"

"怎么躲？它们都住到家里来了。"子卉把老鼠清晨从卧室顶上进来，晚上从厨房顶上出去的整个过程向老公详细描述了一遍。

"我真不敢一个人住在这房子里了。"她细思极恐。

"罗姐能帮忙吗？"老公问。

"帮不了，她比我还怕老鼠。"

"二子可以吗？"子卉的老公想到了二子。

二子是家里养的一只金毛混血狗。老公去北京后，它就是子卉的伴侣。

"二子？你让它狗咬耗子多管闲事？这个年头家猫都不会逮老鼠了，你还指望狗？"和远在万里之外、鞭长莫及的老公废话，让子卉每次都惶然无助。

"那就打电话给除害公司，让他们来处理。"老公提议。

"也只有这样了。"这次是子卉先挂的电话。

子卉知道老公工作忙，他拿了国家投资的钱，公司的里里外外都要事必躬亲。她打电话也就是想舒缓一下心中的焦虑和郁闷，没有更多的奢望。但和老公通电话，是子卉每天必经之事。如果家里平安无事，通常是老公打过来；如果家里出现任何事情，不管发生大事小事，子卉都会抓起电话立刻打过去。

在子卉和老公通话的时间里，二子一般都会坐在旁边。一次，因为什么事，子卉和老公争吵起来，她对着电话歇斯底里地喊叫，吓得二子远远地躲到卧室床底下。从那以后，只要子卉打电话，它都会拉开距离，坐在那儿静静地看着。如果风平浪静，它就摇摇尾巴走过来；如果情况不妙，它就坐在那儿一动不动地盯着子卉。

黑，是一种颜色；暗，是一种状态。对于孤独和恐惧的人来说，黑暗是一种心态。子卉从小就怕黑暗——特别是睡觉前的黑暗。

太阳落下去有一段时间了，黑魆魆的夜幕沉沉地笼罩着整个屋子。子卉像往常一样站起来打开屋里所有的灯。她看到二子仍旧一动不动，目不转睛地盯着自己，就微微向它招了招手。二子低着头慢慢地走过来，卧在子卉的身边。

八年前，子卉领养二子时，它刚好一岁。也是子卉失去飞飞一周年。那一年的春天，子卉意外地发现自已怀孕了。对于结婚五年还没得子的小夫妻真是喜从天降。老公拉着子卉在一家昂贵的高档餐厅好好地搓了一顿，以示庆贺。从那以后，每次下班回到家，他都要摸摸子卉的肚子，看看有没有大一点。子卉都会骄嗔地给他一拳，说："你有没有一点常识？"

这些岁月静好的日子，一直到子卉临产前二个月突然停止。那时子卉是一家公司的会计。年底工作特别忙，每天的超时工作让她疲惫不堪。脚肿得只能穿肥大的拖鞋。老公一直劝她提前休假，她没有听，因为不想失去这份工作。

子卉不会忘记最后一次产检。那是她努力想从记忆中抹去又永远抹不掉的一天。

那天像往常一样，护士安排她换好衣服躺下，等候雷蒙德医生。每月一次的定期产检，子卉都要见他。——一个和蔼幽默的美国老头。温婉的音乐，柔和的灯光，配上墙上各种图片，温馨又详和。每次子卉都很享受躺在这儿等候的这段轻松、愉快的时光。

随着两声敲门声，跟进来的是雷蒙德医生的大嗓门："你好吗？未来的开心妈妈。"

子卉总是给他一个灿烂的笑容。接着他会边开着玩笑边拿出听诊器："快乐的小心脏要蹦出来了！"随着听诊器在圆凸凸的肚子上游走,子卉会听见:"非常好!啊,一切正常!"每次说完这句话,他会像交响乐团的指挥在曲终时做出的一个颇为夸张的动作。

然而,这一次子卉却没有期待到她最熟悉、也是最开心的这句话。放在肚子上的听珍器久久没有拿起来。子卉从来没有见过雷蒙德医生有过这么严肃的表情。

他喃喃地自语:"可能……不太……"

在雷蒙德医生语焉不详的后面,子卉的心突然惶恐不安起来。她用手紧紧地抓住了床沿。

超生波的图像里,黑暗的子宫一片沉寂。蓦然间,子卉惊遽而起,又无力地躺下,一切都明白了。此时的子卉,只能任凭泪水恣意地流淌。

发生的这一切恍若昨日。当时,子卉的大脑一片空白,完全不记得雷蒙德医生说了些什么。没有任何语言可以抚慰这丧子之痛,更痛的是,连下一次机会都没有留下。子宫在引产的大出血中被一道拿掉了,灰飞烟灭。为了怀念这个还没飞翔就夭折的儿子,他们给他起名飞飞。

由祥音切换成噩耗常常发生在瞬间。然而,悲伤只能等待时间之水一点一点地稀释。为了尽快抚平这次的伤痛,在医生的建议下,子卉领养了这条金毛狗。他们给它取名二子,意思就是家里的老二。

在这个"快乐的影子"的陪伴下,低沉多时的子卉一点点收拾起自己残破的心境。

二子有一双善解人意的眼睛,就像子卉的儿子一样时时跟在她的后面。当它发现子卉情绪不佳时,会走过去用前爪轻轻碰一下她,好像在说:想什么呢?有时,它会用嘴推一下子卉的腿，又去碰一下挂在那里的项圈皮带，意思是：别难过了，我们出去走走吧，一切都会过去的。当子卉开心的时候，它会扑过去哚哚子卉的脸，用自己的方式传递喜悦。

子卉常常想，当上天降临痛苦的时候，也会同时给你承受痛苦的力量，这种力量来自于爱。

没过多久，子卉开始了另一个爱好，种花。老公去了北京后，她种得更疯狂了。在绿叶吐芽、花开花落中体会生命的流动，寻找生活的慰藉。

子卉家的后院里，经常会看到她和二子忙碌的身影。她挖坑，它就在边上也刨一个，有时用力过猛把坑刨得太大，她会拍拍它的头说，小子，你帮倒忙了。这时它就高兴地扭着身子摇尾巴。有时它会用嘴衔着花园工具递过来，但又常常递错了，引得子卉直叫。它就兴奋地在院子里从这头跑到那头。

一次，子卉和二子在一条小路上散步，一只蜗牛正缓慢地在他们面前爬行。它跑过去嗅了嗅，用嘴轻轻把蜗牛拱到路边，再跑回子卉身边 。子卉用力地拥抱它。

因为有二子，子卉感到无比幸运；也因为二子，子卉没有去北京。她知道就是去了北京，和老公也一样是聚少离多。老公一直都认为自己有一种使命。子卉却不以为然，我们没有什么使命，没有人有使命。人只能在这个世界上走上一次，没有人能验证哪一条路是正确的。

第二天早晨刚过上班时间，子卉的电话就打到了"除害"公司，约好下午有人过来。她希望把这些老鼠赶走而不是杀害。公司来的人说，这是世界性的问题，老鼠一旦定居下来，要想赶走是一件很难的事，尤其在阁楼上。我们负责用最好最快的办法来清除它们。

三天过后，头顶上渐渐趋于平静。子卉有一种久违的轻松。

晚上，天黑没多久，后院响起一阵阵低沉的哀鸣。子卉拉开门。在一泓淡淡的月光下，二子横卧在草地的尽头，它睁大的眼睛里充满痛苦。看见子卉出来，它颤颤巍巍地站了起来，摇摇晃晃没走几步，前腿一软，又瘫在地上。

子卉几步冲到它的面前。它向子卉投去疲惫的一瞥，然后又吃力地摇了摇尾巴。子卉知道，它在和自己说话。

"二子！二子！你怎么了？"子卉大声喊道。

二子无力地眨了眨眼，仿佛很抱歉自己没能坚强些。

子卉用力抱起它。瞬间，手上便沾满了黏糊糊的液体。借着月光，她看见了血，强烈的血腥味迅速弥漫在空气中。此刻，血正从二子身下无保留地泻了下来。子卉嗅到了恐怖的气息。她再也忍不住了，号啕恸哭。

哭声惊动了邻居。他们和后来赶到的罗姐把二子送到了兽医急诊所。

子卉心里害怕到了极点。满脑子都是二子渐渐衰耗的眼神。她茫然地盯着抢救室的门，心里不停地祈祷。

罗姐安慰着子卉。她深有体会男人长期不在身边是什么滋味。

医生终于出来了，带来了不好不坏的消息：好的是二子还活着，正在抢救；不好的是还不能确定何时才能脱离危险。它是鼠药中毒，死亡率很高。

这时子卉才意识到发生了什么。她恨自己没有考虑周全。

回到家已经是午夜了。屋子里一片死寂。子卉很久没有体验这种感觉了。她怀念起以前曾经厌恶的那种窸窸窣窣的声音，至少它能带来一些生命的气息。

打往北京的电话通了，子卉这边鸦雀无声。此刻她不想说话，她太累了。她也怕自己崩溃，怕自己忍不住喊叫，怕喊出出格的话。

老公不知道这边怎么了。为什么电话接通了又没人说话？他急了，不断地嚷："喂，喂，子卉，子卉，是你吗？说话呀！"

他怕子卉此刻犯了心脏病，他怕她此刻气管被东西卡住。他更怕此刻她遭人绑架。

啜泣声慢慢由小变大，转瞬变成哀嚎。这暴风骤雨般的哭声，让她把这几年积攒起来的孤独、忧伤、痛苦和思念一股脑地砸了过去。老公猝不及防。

她说，她不能忍受那种强颜笑面后的牵肠挂肚；更不能忍受夜阑人静后面的孤枕难眠。她不要这种残缺的生活。她仅仅想要一个完整的家！

电话那头，老公沉默了。

他知道这些年子卉形单影只、惶然无助地生活在美国。可是，他还是不明白自己有什么错；为了这个家，自己在外面闯在外面拚。为了拚出更好的日子，自己也常常徘徊在各种压力和苦闷中。

电话两头都沉默了。

他一直让子卉耐心地等候——等候更好的日子，等候辉煌的一天。仿佛这样才对得起自己的人生，对得起这个家。

子卉不这么认为。她认为没有比这种等候更无意义，更让人绝望。因为这种等候是痛苦的。

他认为子卉的困难并不会比别人多太多；这些痛苦都是来自于内心的骄弱。他要她学会忍耐，把自己变得更坚强。

子卉认为，来自身体的痛苦可以忍受，自己是个能吃苦的人。但就是不明白为何要制造这种人为的精神痛苦？活着这么简单。为什么不能在满足基本生活需要后，从容地享受生活。

他则认为，活着的目的就是要比别人活得好，让别人仰慕，让别人嫉妒。这就是锣鼓、鞭炮在中国从古至今的作用。

子卉则认为这是一个陷井。它在迷惑我们，引诱我们往下跳。

子卉麻木了。她无力地靠在沙发上，不在听，也不想说……

大门外传来一阵挠门的响声和低低的狗吠，声音很熟悉。子卉一阵狂喜。她奔过去用力拉开门。是二子！它直直地坐在门前，眼睛死死盯着子卉，尾巴拖在后面一动不动，没有往常的开心。子卉蹲下身去抱它，瞬间呆住了。一群老鼠正围坐在二子的周围，用同样的眼神盯着自己。她大惊失色，快速退回门内。老鼠却赶在她关门之前一个个挤了进来。不多不少正好八只。子卉吓得夺门而出。这时，手机铃响了。

放在沙发尽头的手机已经响了好几声了。子卉一骨碌从沙发上爬起来，她迷迷糊糊地抓起电话。电话是兽医打来的。医生告诉子卉,通过洗胃、灌肠和注射药物,二子已经基本脱离了危险。只是还需要再观察两天。

天已大亮了。子卉打开了前门,迎着刺眼的阳光,她深深地吸了一口气。

DISLOCATION

~

*E*arly in the morning, before dawn, the sound above the corner of the bedroom wall appeared again. It was a rustling noise, just audible, punctuated by a pause measured in seconds. Zihui counted in silence; the sound recurred eight times.

The noise had exhausted Zihui lately. It was odd, but with a consistent pattern. She'd first heard it in the kitchen. It was getting dark that evening. As she sat at the table drinking tea, a slight yet clear noise of friction sounded over her head in the quiet room. At first, she didn't pay much attention to it. Perhaps it was the wind. However, the noise returned over the next few days, always with the same pattern. She counted carefully: eight times at a time.

It frightened Zihui. When the last rustling was over, she

could no longer hold her breath and grabbed the phone to call Beijing. Her husband was in a meeting.

Her voice trembled and jerked around as she told him what had spooked her. Her husband was patient, listening to her for a while, but he still couldn't understand what happened at home.

"I have an important meeting here today," he said. "I really don't have time. You go find Sister Luo." Then he hung up.

Her husband had gone to Beijing three years ago after quitting a dull job he'd held in the States for over ten years. He'd left resolutely.

Zihui and Sister Luo lived in the same neighborhood. Luo had come to the States from Wuhan, China, to accompany her son. She'd had more free time since her son had entered junior high school. The women, both of whose husbands were away from home, soon got together.

"It's easy," said Luo. "You stay inside. I'll be waiting outside the house. When you hear the noise, text me."

In the evening, before it was completely dark, Luo crouched behind a lilac bush in the backyard of Zihui's house, staring at the kitchen roof, where the sound came from, according to Zihui. She listened with bated breath, waiting for Zihui to send a text.

A little later, Luo's cell phone vibrated. Sure enough, something loomed up above. It was a large rat, peeping out from the corner of the roof over the kitchen. Luo held her breath and widened her eyes. The first one, who twisted her head a few times as if to spy on the surroundings, should be the leader. A few seconds later, one after the other, they filed out in the dim dusk.

Luo's heart raced. All women were afraid of rats, and Luo was no exception. The mice seen in China were two or three inches long, while the rats here looked like little kittens. She tallied them one by one, eight in all. They hissed over the rooftop and vanished in the blink of an eye.

Luo told Zihui what she'd seen; Zihu was dumbfounded.

SHE HAD DREADED three things since she was a kid: rats, dead people, and the dark. She remembered that the three often appeared at the same time in a movie scene. Father and husband both laughed at her. *What is to fear from the dead? Living people are more terrible.* However, Zihui wasn't apprehensive about the living. As a kid, she'd fought with the naughtiest boys. She was frightened of the dead because she couldn't comprehend why a person wouldn't move any longer. From an early age, her father had told her that everyone would die anyway, regardless of how awesome they were; however, he didn't clarify where people would go after death. It was dreadful because nobody knew, she concluded.

Zihui now understood what the noise was that she heard in the ceiling of the bedroom early in the morning—it was the rats, at least eight of them, living in the attic above her head. A big family had come here uninvited.

She called Beijing again.

Her husband was impatient. "Isn't it just a rat? Could a

rat scare such a big person? As the saying goes, cowardly like a rat. The rats are at the bottom of the food chain. What are you afraid of?"

Rationally, Zihui understood; however, a fear was still a fear. Barely any ladies weren't afraid of rats. Zihui could list off a series of reasons: they were despicable, dirty, ugly, and sneaky. When you bumped into them, they ran away in a frenzy, making you feel creepy.

The husband said, "Their nocturnal nature is given to them by God, and we shouldn't blame them. They can't help themselves."

"Stop it. That's easy for you to say."

"You each mind your own business, and you can just ignore them."

"How? They all live in our house." Zihui described the whole process of rats rolling in the attic of the bedroom in the morning and going out from the attic of the kitchen in the evening.

"I don't dare to live in this house alone." She was scaring herself to death.

"Would Sister Luo be able to help?" asked the husband.

"No, she's more afraid of rats than I am."

"How about Erzi?"

Erzi—meaning "the second son"—was a golden retriever, Zihui's companion since her husband had gone to Beijing.

"Erzi? You want a dog to chase the rats? It's not his business. Domestic cats can't even catch mice these days, and you expect a dog will do that?" Jabbering nonsense on the phone with her husband thousands of miles away made Zihui feel helpless each time.

"Call a pest control company and let them handle it," her husband suggested. "That's all we can do." This time, Zihui hung up on her husband first.

Zihui knew her husband was occupied with his work, which was funded by government investment. He had to attend to everything inside and outside the company. The phone calls were to ease her anxiety and depression, with no extravagant hopes. But chatting on the phone with her husband was a daily necessity for Zihui. If everything was all right, her husband would call her. Otherwise, in case anything happened at home, no matter how big or small, Zihui would grab the phone and call right away.

Whenever Zihui and her husband talked to each other, Erzi often sat alongside her. Once, Zihui had screamed at the phone when she and her husband were quarreling over something; scared, Erzi had hidden far underneath her bed. Since then, as soon as Zihui got on the phone, he would pull away and sit there watching. If the conversation went smoothly, he'd wag his tail and come closer; if the situation wasn't going well, he'd not move, just sit there gazing at her.

BLACK WAS A COLOR; darkness was a state. For those who were lonely and fearful, it was a state of mind. Zihui had been afraid of the dark since childhood—before bedtime in particular.

The sun had set some time ago, and the dark night hung

over the whole house. Zihui stood up to turn on all the lights in the house as usual. Seeing Erzi was still motionless, staring at her, she beckoned to him. He crept up with his head down and lay beside Zihui.

Erzi had been exactly one year old when Zihui had adopted him eight years ago. It was also one year after Zihui had lost Feifei. That spring, Zihui had found herself pregnant. It was a surprise to the couple, who had been married for five years. Her husband had taken Zihui to an upscale restaurant to celebrate. After that, every time he came home from work, he wanted to feel Zihui's belly to see if the baby had grown bigger. Zihui would give him a punch with pride and said, "Do you have any common sense?"

The quiet days of those years had come to an abrupt end two months before Zihui's expected labor. Zihui was an accountant at her company. She was very busy around the end of the year and was exhausted from working late every day. Her feet were so swollen that she could only wear loose slippers. Her husband had urged her to take off early, but she had no choice; she didn't want to lose her job.

Zihui would never forget the last prenatal examination. It was a day she'd tried to erase from her memory but never could.

As usual, the nurse had told her to change, lie down and wait for Dr. Raymond, a kind and humorous American old man with whom she met once a month for regular checkups. Gentle music, soft lighting, and various pictures on the wall created a warm and peaceful space. Zihui always enjoyed the relaxing and happy time she spent lying there and waiting for the doctor.

Two knocks would come, followed by Dr. Raymond's loud voice: "How are you? Happy mother at last."

Zihui would give a splendid smile. Then, as usual, Dr. Raymond would pull out his stethoscope. "Happy little heart is about to pop out!" he'd jest. As the stethoscope roamed over the bulging belly, Zihui would always hear, "Superb! Ah, everything is normal!" He'd act like a conductor at the end of a symphony with an exaggerated gesture each time as he said that.

However, Zihui didn't hear the familiar and pleasing words she expected this time. The stethoscope stayed on her belly for quite a while. Zihui had never seen Dr. Raymond look so serious.

He mumbled to himself, "Perhaps... no..."

Hearing Dr. Raymond's ambiguous words, Zihui panicked. She clutched the edges of the examining table.

In the ultrasound image, the dark uterus was silent. Zihui understood everything. She jumped up in shock and then lay down, impaired. She could only let her tears flow at will.

All this felt like yesterday. Zihui's mind was blank, and she couldn't remember what Dr. Raymond had said. No language could soothe the agony of losing a child, but what was more agonizing was not being given another chance. The doctor had removed her womb amid the massive bleeding in the induced labor. To remember the son who had died before being able to "fei"—the Chinese word for *fly*—they had given him a name: Feifei.

THE CHANGE from an auspicious voice to tragic news often occurred in an instant. However, the sorrow could only wait for the water of time to dilute it little by little. To heal the pain as quickly as possible, Zihui had adopted this golden retriever on the advice of the doctor. She'd named him Erzi because he was the second "kid" in the family.

Accompanied by this "happy shadow," Zihui's mood had recovered slowly after a prolonged depression.

Erzi had a pair of kind eyes and followed Zihui around like her little boy. When Zihui was in a bad mood, he'd come up, caressing her with his front paws, as if to say, "What are you thinking?" Sometimes, he'd push Zihui's legs with his mouth and then touch his leash where it hung from the wall, as if telling her, "Don't be sad. Let's go out for a walk, and everything will be fine." When Zihui was upbeat, he'd jump over to lick her face, sharing her joy in his own way.

Zihui often thought that when God delivered pain, he'd also give you the power to endure it, which came from love.

Not long after, Zihui had taken up another hobby, gardening. The new passion grew even stronger after her husband went to Beijing. It let her feel the flow of life and seek comfort in watching the plants sprout and the flowers bloom.

She and Erzi were often busy working together in the

backyard. When Zihui dug a pit, Erzi would also dig one off to the side. Sometimes he worked too hard, making the hole too large. Zihui would pat his head and said, "Boy, you're counterproductive." Erzi would twist his body and wag his tail happily. Sometimes he'd hold a garden tool in his mouth and bring it to her, but often he got the wrong one, causing Zihui to holler. Ecstatic at the moment, he would run in the backyard from end to end.

Once, when Zihui and Erzi were walking along a trail, a snail crawled in front of them. Erzi ran to sniff it and tenderly carried the snail to the side of the road with his mouth. Zihui gave him a big hug when he ran back to her.

Zihui felt so fortunate to have Erzi that she didn't go to Beijing because of him. She knew even if she was there, she and her husband wouldn't be able to spend much time together. Her husband always thought he had a mission to complete. Zihui dissented. *We have no mission. No one has a mission. We only walk on this planet once. Nobody can verify which way is right.*

THE FOLLOWING MORNING, Zihui called the pest control company and made an appointment for the afternoon. She'd have liked to drive the rats away, as opposed to killing them. The guy from the company said it was a worldwide problem, and once the rats had settled down, it was hard to get rid of them, especially in the attic. "We'll eradicate them in the best and quickest way possible."

After three days, the noise overhead gradually died down. Zihui got her long-lost tranquility back.

Soon after dark that evening, a murmur of distress came from the backyard. Zihui opened the door. Erzi lay at the edge of the grass under the faint moonlight, his eyes wide open with pain. Seeing Zihui come out, he trembled, trying to stand up. He wobbled for a few steps before his front legs weakened and he toppled to the ground.

She rushed to him. Erzi threw a tired glance at her and then painfully wagged his tail. Zihui knew he was talking to her.

"Erzi! Erzi, what's the matter with you?" Zihui shouted.

Erzi blinked feebly, as if he was sorry for not being stronger.

Zihui pulled him to her. In the instant, her hands were covered with a sticky liquid. In the moonlight, she saw it was blood, and its strong scent soon permeated the air. The blood poured from under his body. Zihui smelled of terror. She couldn't resist wailing.

The cry alarmed the neighbors. They and Sister Luo, who arrived later, took Erzi to the vet's emergency care.

Zihui was frightened. Her mind was full of Erzi's fading eyes. She gazed at the door of the emergency room, praying in her heart.

Luo kept comforting Zihui. She knew well what it was like to have your man away for a long time.

The doctor came out at last and brought the could-go-either-way news. The good news was Erzi was still alive and being treated, while the bad news was that it was unclear when he might be out of danger. Rodenticides had poisoned him, and the death rate was high.

Zihui realized what had happened. She hated herself for not being thoughtful.

It was midnight before she returned home. The house was dead silent. Zihui hadn't experienced this feeling for a while. She missed the noise she had hated before, the rustling from the rats, which, at least, could bring a breath of life.

The call to Beijing went through, but Zihui was quiet. She didn't want to talk now as she was excessively drained. Also, she feared that she'd break down, that she couldn't resist shouting and scolding, acting out of line.

Her husband didn't know what had happened at home. Why did she not speak after the phone was connected? "Hello? Hello? Zihui? Zihui, is that you? Say something!" he kept shouting.

He worried that Zihui might be having a heart attack, or she might be choking. He was even more fearful of her being abducted.

The sobs grew gradually louder and then turned into a howl in an instant. With a wild roar, she let out the loneliness, sadness, torment, and yearning amassed over the years all at once, catching her husband off guard.

She said she couldn't stand the anxiety hidden behind her smiling face and couldn't endure the sleepless nights on the lonely pillow. She didn't want this kind of partial life. All she wanted was a complete family !

Her husband was quiet at the other end of the call.

He knew Zihui had been living alone in the States all these years without a helping hand. Still, he didn't understand what was wrong with himself. *I was also trying hard to improve life for the family and often dealt with pressure and anguish*, he thought.

It was quiet on both ends now.

He had been letting Zihui wait patiently for a better day, a brilliant day, as if this was the only way to fulfill his own dreams and those of the family.

Zihui didn't think this way. She believed that nothing was more meaningless and desperate than this kind of waiting, because it was painful.

He reckoned Zihui faced no more challenges than others did; her despair originated from her inner weakness. He told her to be patient and strong.

Zihui thought that pain inside the body could be endured, and she was a person who could bear hardship. But why should this kind of artificial mental misery be created? *Life is so straightforward. Why can't we take time to enjoy life after our basic daily needs are satisfied?*

He believed the motivation behind living was to be superior to others, to be admired and envied by others. This was the role of drums and firecrackers in China from ancient times to the present.

Zihui thought this was a trap. *It's deceiving us and tempting us to jump into it.*

. . .

Zihui was numb. She leaned feebly on the couch, not listening, not wanting to say anything…

Outside the front door came a familiar scratching noise and a low barking. Zihui was overjoyed. She rushed to open the door. *It's Erzi!* He sat right in front of the door, his eyes fixed on Zihui, his tail trailing behind him. He was motionless and didn't look as upbeat as usual. Zihui crouched down and wanted to hug him. In that moment, she froze. A group of rats sat around Erzi, staring at her with the same eyes. She was stunned and sprinted back. The rats crowded in one by one before she could close the door. No more, no less, just eight. Zihui dashed out in fear. At that point the phone rang.

Her cell phone at the end of the couch had already rung several times. Zihui rolled off the couch and snatched up the phone in a daze. The call was from the vet, who told Zihui that Erzi was out of danger. They'd cleaned his stomach and intestines and injected him with medication. They'd still need to observe him for two more days, said the vet.

It was already bright outside. Zihui opened the front door and drew a deep breath in the dazzling sunlight.

异乡

这是爸妈第三次来美国。第一次来的时候,我还没有孩子,利用暑假时间带着他们转了大半个美国。第二次他们是来帮我做月子的。这次是来照顾他们的小外孙,好让我安心上班。

我在国内学的是中文专业,三年前在美国高中谋到了一个教中文的职位。——它看起来不起眼,可还是需要过硬的英文和以前教中文的经验。能从几十个候选的中国人中荣幸地被选中,让我很珍惜这个工作机会。

课程有限,挣钱不多,美国高中生也不好管理,但是我还是很喜欢这份工作,主要是因为学校有寒暑假。在这三、四个月的时间里,我可以做很多自己想做的事情。

爸妈来的这个时间离我暑期结束还有两个星期。为了尽快让他们和小外孙熟悉起来,我包揽了家里的其他事情。

一岁的儿子大头大脑，很顽皮。加上小家伙处在学走路的阶段，照顾他是一件又好玩、又辛苦的事。爸妈来了以后，我多出不少时间。只要有空，我就会躲在书房里看书、写作。他们有时会进来和我聊上一会儿，不外乎讲一些亲戚、邻居和他们朋友中的一些事情。其实这些在过去来来回回的电话里都已经说过。不过每次他们说起来，我还是显得饶有兴趣。

最近几次，我注意到他们俩总想对我说什么，却欲言又止，而且都是在他们分别和我谈话的时候。我明白了，一定有什么事困扰着他们。

记得在我上高中的时候，有个男生和我比较要好；我们也算不上谈恋爱。他只去过我家一次。那天我俩走在一起时正巧被我爸碰见。晚饭后，他们俩非常正式地和我整整谈了一个小时，把古今中外因为过早谈恋爱而毁了自己的例子举了个遍。在整个过程中，我都没吭声。他们俩你一句，我一句讲得有声有色。总结成一句话，就是为了我好。谈话在我歇斯底里的大喊声中结束。这一声是我有生以来喊得最疯狂、也是最悲壮的。把他们吓得不轻。首先，我郑重地告诉他们，那些都不是事实。再就是，对他们不管多大的事都轮流教训我的方式特别反感，这是把孩子逼着跳楼的最好的方式。从那以后，他们还真改掉了一起上阵教训我的习惯。

昨天早晨我爸终于问到了主题上："学校能挣多少钱？"

"不多，因为我教的不是主流课程，本来在美国学校里教书就挣得不多。"

"那你没想改变一下？"

"怎么变？"

"学点别的什么？比如说计算机。我也不是太懂。"

"你好像很懂。"我这话说得不太好听。

"你在西雅图的表妹,就是那个以前在国内学法语,来美国后又改学计算机的。据说她挣得不错。每次你小姨打电话来都是那种兴奋的语调,说完总要顺带问问你,好像满同情我们的。"

我开始露出了一些不耐烦。我当然知道这个表妹;只是来往不多。最近她好像当上了公司部门主管。她是属于那种在美国很能混的类型:见人能夸张地像美国人那样拥抱、说笑。再不喜欢你,她也能装出一种喜欢和欣赏你的模样。即使倒下去了,她也有能爬起来住上攀的毅力。这些都属于"职业情商"。

我爸说我是嫉妒。我告诉他,不是每个人都喜欢那种生活的。

学校开学了。由于和中国做生意的美国公司越来越多,美国人学中文的热情似乎也高涨起来。这学期学校每周又给我加了几堂课。我比以前忙碌了一些。

班上学中文的学生中,中国孩子和白人孩子大约各占到一半。中国孩子的中文大部分都略高于我授课的水平。他们从小混在各种周末中文学校里,这种不间断地学习让他们打下了不错的基础。说白了,他们到我这儿来也只是为了混个高分,以利于申请更好的大学。白人的孩子多数是好奇,有些是听从家长的建议来试着学学看的。

中国孩子在白人教师那里通常表现得都很乖,可到了我这儿却一反常态。他们明显有一种莫名的优越感,这大概来自于能比白人孩子多讲几句中文,或是把我这个在美国中学老师里罕见的中国人当成了"自己人"。

珊蒂是我们班里一个混血儿。妈妈是日本人，爸爸是个人高马大的美国白人。她学中文的最大动力就是能和从中国收养来的妹妹保持中文沟通。她说，爸爸妈妈不想让妹妹忘记自己是中国人。我曾经问过她为什么不学日语呀；她想了想说，好像觉得没有什么用。

我在班上也问过其它孩子学中文的目的。白人孩子有的说"酷"，有的干脆就说不知道。反正高中要求学一门第二语言，学什么都一样。中国孩子的目标似乎要高一些。因为中国发展快，如果能懂中文，今后会有更多的机会。

教书是一份钱少而又辛苦的职业。就看你想要什么了。正好这就是我想要并喜欢的。

星期六的早晨，老公一早就去公司加班了。做为一名工程师，他比我要忙很多。

吃过早饭，收拾好屋子，看儿子东东没醒，我坐下来想看一会儿书。自从有了孩子，我学会见缝插针。

爸妈前后走了进来。

我妈问："周末还干活呢？"

我答："是自己的事。"

我爸说："等你有空了我们再聊。"

我说："爸妈，没事，你们坐吧。时间吧，要说没有也没有，要说有也有，在美国就是这样。"

我看得出，他们住在这里有些拘谨，特别是我老公在家的时候。其实，我老公是个热情好客的人，对我父母也很好。只是老人住在儿女家不像住在自己家那么自在。

我把打开的书合了起来。平时忙的没顾上,周末真的应该陪他们说说话。

我妈说:"每次来美国,最大的感觉就是寂寞。出门看不见几个人,时间久了,心里觉得慌慌的。"

我说:"是呀,我来这么久了也还没习惯呢。特别是待在家里时间长了,真像是与世隔绝。所以美国很多老人到了退休年龄也不敢退休,一是钱不够,再就是怕孤独。"

"在美国多大年龄可以退休?"我爸问。

"按能拿社会保障养老金算,目前男女都是六十六岁。以后也许还会推迟。到了我这个年龄,能不能拿到还不知道呢。"我说。

我妈瞪大眼睛说:"真要等那么晚? 我们中国可不就是女的五十五,男的六十就都退休了。美国是全世界最有钱的地方。怎么会是这样?"

"这些事要说起来就复杂了。每个国家的国情不一样。"我不想讲的太多。这个话题能说上大半天呢。讲多了吧,他们又要说来美国是个错误的选择。我知道他们很想让我们回国,来过几次他们都没有喜欢上这里。

我爸说:"我们每天除了照顾东东做做家务,几乎没有别的活动。"

我妈说:"关健是不开车哪里都去不了。不像我们在家里,公交车和地铁四通八达,乘车到那儿都行。而且老人还免费。"

我爸同情地看了我妈一眼说:"上班时间四处静悄悄的,每当有辆车经过,你妈都会扭头朝窗外看。等你们下班了又各忙各的。真正能坐在一起说说话的时间很少。时间久了还真感到寂寞。"

听了这些话我心里感到一阵愧疚,连忙说:"真是对不起。最近这段时间我们俩都太忙,没有顾及到您们的感受。今后周末有时间,一定经常带您们出去转转。"

我妈说:"你们这里也没什么好转的。人人出门都坐在铁壳车里。马路上连个人影都看不到,只有买东西的地方还能见到几个人。不像我们那儿满大街都是人。光是站在路边看人都是一种消遣。"

我妈说得没错。做为一个正常人都会有这种感受。

我爸问:"那年纪大了怎么出门?"

"自己开车。"

"那到八十岁呢?"

"要想出门也要自己开。"

我给他们讲了我几年前的一次经历。那天下着小雨,路上有些滑。我是一个开车特别小心的人。到了十字路口时正好是黄灯,我踩了刹车。就在车子刚停稳的那一刻,"嘭"的一声,我的车被追尾了。车子被震得乱晃,向前顶了几步。幸好我前面没车;不然我就成了三明治了。回头一看,后面撞我的是一辆颇大的美国车。我下了车,站在原地等司机出来。正当我疑惑的时候,车门慢慢地开了,一根拐杖从车门下面颤颤巍巍地伸了出来。我定神一看,是一个很老的白人老头,看起来至少有八十岁。他努力地想从座位上站起来,试了两次都没成功。我赶紧过去帮了他一把。他一下抓住我的手哀求道,我可以私下给你钱,求求你千万不要告诉保险公司。如果让他们知道我又出车祸了,就再也不能开车出来买东西了。听了这番话,我心里很不是滋味。因为车子并没有被撞得怎么样,就让他走了。我始终都没有忘记他谢我时眼眶里噙着的泪花。

我妈深深地叹了口气。

我爸想说什么，看了看我妈。我妈给他递了个眼色，他又咽回去了。

我说："爸，你有什么就直说，是不是又想让我改学计算机？"

"也不完全是。其实我们上次来的时候就想说了，正好赶上你坐月子，也就没有提。我们的意思是，"他停顿了一下又说，"我和你妈都觉得你们的日子过得挺清苦的，住的地方又很寂寞。就是希望你们多努努力，多挣些钱，争取今后搬到城里去。"

晚上睡觉前，我把我爸的话说给老公听，他笑得半天都直不起腰来。他很感兴趣我是怎么回答的。我能怎么说？不就是美国地大，人人有车，郊区的别墅宽敞舒适，有自己的院子和车库，加上学区好，犯罪率又低。老公说，总结得还挺全面。他又说，其实你只要告诉他们，我们是有钱人，住的是美国的"大耗子"。"大耗子"都在"乡下"。

我瞪了他一眼："你觉得他们会相信吗？"

听到我们讲大耗子，坐在小床上的东东"咯咯"地笑起来了，嘴里还不断地重复着大耗子、大耗子。他是属鼠的，手边有一堆大大小小的老鼠玩具。

我们买的"大耗子"是全新的。这房子是我和老公看着工人们盖起来的。有个周末，我俩坐在工地上整整看了二个小时。建房的速度之快让我们目瞪口呆，简直就像在搭积木。横竖交接的细木条上，只敲上几根钉子。早晨才从地基上盖起，晚上整个屋架就搭好了。当时老公问我："美国龙卷风这么多，你敢住吗？"

"不敢！"我回答得很肯定。"可是头款已付了。不住这里，我们住哪儿？"

整个美国的住房都是这么盖起来的。里面包上一拳就能打通的石膏板；外面盖上塑料板条，高档一些的会糊上一层薄灰泥或者贴上些"面子砖"。几十年后再回来看看，整个小区一片衰败。前一阵子，老公给我看了一张他的一个同事家房子的照片。贴在房子正面的一大片装饰石块突然坍塌，一片狼藉。

这是快餐经济的一部分。这样的房子还有一个名字叫"伪豪宅"。老公经常说，我们用买豪宅的价钱，买了个伪豪宅。情何以堪！

这个周末，老公没去加班。我们带着我爸我妈去了一家略为高档的意大利餐厅。去得早，人还不算多。我们挑了一个安静的角落坐了下来。东东坐在专为婴儿设置的高椅上。他这个年龄正在学说话，见到生人就"哇哇"叫个不停。

老公把领位小姐递过来的菜单放在我爸妈面前。

"你明知道我是个睁眼瞎。"我妈有些为难地说。

"菜单上有些菜有照片，可以参考一下。"老公很热情，"我来念，你们来选。"

意大利饮食其实也没有太多的花样——各式的面条，不同的彼萨饼和各种沙拉菜。老公耐心地一一推荐。

"面条？"我妈摇摇头，"面条有什么好吃的？没空做饭才下面条吃。到餐馆还吃面条？"

"这是意大利面条，也叫意粉。"老公特意加上了意大利几个字。"加的佐料不一样，是西式的。"

"好吧，那就试试。"我妈妥协了。

最后，我们各样都点了一些。

东东坐在他的高椅上，一手抓着一块彼萨，吃得满脸都是红红的西红柿酱。他一边吃一边摇头晃脑地哼唱着。其他人都很安静。

吃了一会儿，老公试着打开话题："我们这个小家庭虽然没有发财，也算是个殷实的家庭。"

"我们来了几趟后也知道在美国真的不容易。"我爸说，"工作不稳定，退休又那么晚。以后能省还是要省。今天这顿大概又要吃掉不少钱吧？说句实话，这面条还没你妈做的炸酱面好吃。"

我妈笑着说："挺好吃的，很浓的奶油香味。老头吃不惯西餐，就胡乱讲。"她接着又说："我想起上次我们来时吃的那个中国餐馆。还记得你们临走时放在桌上的二十块钱吗？当时我就悄悄地对你爸说，在美国吃餐馆真便宜，这么一桌菜才二十块钱。回国后我又说给你小姨听，被她笑成土包子。我这才知道，那二十块只是付的小费。"

我们都笑了。东东也拍着两只油乎乎的小手"哇啦哇啦"乱叫。

笑过以后，我爸严肃地对我老公说："上次我和亦婷说过一次，建议她去学计算机，还年青嘛。"

我一直以为他只是随便说说，没想到他是认真的。

"知道你从小就喜欢文学。"我爸又对着我说，"但是我一直都有看法。"他用大拇指搓搓中指和食指说，"现在成功就是这个。你们可能认为俗气，可现实生活就是这样。符合社会习俗就是对的，反之就是错的。现在谁还看那些闲书？大家都讲学以至用，用不到学它干嘛？小说都是编造的，有什么好看好写的？"

一阵沉默。

我妈看气氛有些紧张，连忙说："你爸也是为你们好。"说完，看看我老公。

我有些惊愕地看着他们。知道这番话的背后肯定有一个故事。我想一定是我的这份工作，让他们在和亲戚朋友的对话、攀比中，伤了埋在深处的那条虚荣神经。

老公说："爸说得没错。现在这个社会已经被物质化了，有钱就是英雄。可是物质富俗的代价不应该是精神的贫穷。"他停了一下，看我爸没说什么，又说："您们也不要太操心亦婷。她写的小说挺有味道的。你们有空可以读读。我很羡慕她有这么一个爱好，又有个喜欢的工作。钱嘛，够用就行。"

我从心里很感激老公。其实，我们这个时代的绝大多数人都在照猫画虎，不管白猫还是黑猫。

我一直没有说话。我不想让他们认为我是一个不孝顺的女儿。然而，我也真的不愿意驮着长辈的期望生活；把孝顺他们，让他们开心做为我生命的终极目的。

离开餐厅的时候，我妈看我没有在桌上放钱，悄悄地提醒我。我说，上次是在中国餐馆，我怕老板苛扣服务生的小费。这次我把小费放在信用卡上了。

A STRANGE LAND

~

This is my parents' third visit to the States. I had no child when they first came here, so I took them to visit many places around the country amid summer vacation. The second time they came was to help me with the postnatal days. This time they come to care for their little grandson, so I can work at ease.

After graduating college in China with a major in Chinese Literature, I got a position teaching Chinese at an American high school—which sounds unremarkable, yet it required good English skills, and experience teaching Chinese. I'm honored to have been chosen from dozens of Chinese candidates, making me cherish this job opportunity.

Despite a limited curriculum, not making much money, and having to manage American high school students, which is not all that simple, I like the job a lot because of the school's summer and winter breaks. I'm free to do what I want during these three to four months.

My parents arrived just two weeks before the end of summer break. To let them get acquainted with their little grandson as quickly as possible, I've been taking care of everything else at home.

My son is one year old, with a big head, and very naughty. Since the little guy is at the stage of learning to walk, dealing with him is both fun and tiring. Since my parents came, I have more spare time and hide in my study to read and write whenever I get a chance. They sometimes come in to chat about their relatives, neighbors, and friends, as they did in our back-and-forth phone calls in the past. Still, I make sure to act interested every time.

Lately, I've noticed that the two of them will seem like they're trying to say something but will wind up saying nothing. Also, it's only happened when they're in my room separately. I understand there must be something troubling them.

I recall I had a guy companion in high school; we weren't yet in a relationship. He'd only been to my home once. My father ran into us as we were strolling together that day, which prompted my parents to have a formal conversation with me for an hour after dinner. Taking cases from ancient and present-day China and also foreign countries, they laid out how individuals ruined themselves by falling in love too soon. I said nothing while they were going back and forth, making their points. To sum it up, it was for my own good. The conversation ended with my insane yelling, the craziest and most distressed cry I had ever uttered. They were frightened. First, I solemnly stated that none of their presumptions was valid. In addition, no matter how big a deal something was, it disgusted me particularly when they tried to lecture me together by taking turns, as this would be the best way to force your child to jump off a building. From that point onward, they broke the habit of playing together at instructing me.

Yesterday morning, my dad finally touched on the topic they'd been avoiding. "How much money can you earn at that school?"

"Not much, because it's not a mainstream program, and teaching in American schools doesn't pay much."

"Then you don't want to change that?"

"How?"

"Learn something else, like the computer. I know little about it."

"You seem to know a lot." I didn't say it nicely.

"Your cousin in Seattle, the one who studied French at home, switched to the computer when she came to America. It's said she makes a lot. Every time your auntie calls, she tells us that in an excited voice, and then asks about you, as if she feels sorry for us."

My impatience began to show. Obviously, I know this cousin; however, I've had little interaction with her. She seems to have become the head of one of her company's departments recently. She is one of those people who can blend well in America. When meeting people, she'll hug them and giggle in an exaggerated way like Americans. On the off chance she doesn't care for you, she can still put on a show of loving and appreciating you. Even if she falls down, she has the willpower to stand up and continue the climb. These are all part of "occupational EQ."

My dad said I'm jealous. I told him that not everyone enjoys that kind of life.

School starts. As more companies in the States do business with China, Americans' enthusiasm for learning Chinese has appeared to rise. The school has added a few more classes for me this term. I'm a little busier than before.

About half of the students in this class are Chinese, and half are white. Most Chinese children speak at a slightly higher level than I'm instructing. They grew up attending the weekend Chinese schools, and this kind of continuous learning has laid a good foundation for them. To put it bluntly, they come to get high scores, so they can apply for a good university. White children are mostly inquisitive and want to give it a shot after their parents' recommendation.

Chinese youngsters, who're usually timid before white teachers, reverse their attitude and display a palpable sense of superiority that probably comes from being able to speak more Chinese than white children. Another possibility is that they consider me, a rare Chinese among American high school teachers, as one of their own.

Sandy is a half-breed in the class. Her mother is Japanese, and her father is a big white man. Her biggest motivation to learn Chinese is to be able to communicate with her adopted sister from China. "My parents don't want my sister to forget that she's Chinese," she said. I once asked her why she doesn't learn Japanese; she said it seems to have little use.

I also asked other children in class about the purpose of learning Chinese. Some white kids said, "It's cool"; the others said, "I don't know." Anyway, high school requires learning a second language, regardless of what language you pick. Chinese children seem to have higher objectives. China is growing fast. You'll have more opportunities if you can master Chinese.

A teacher's job is one of diligent work for little money. It depends on what you want. All things considered, this is what I need and like.

ON SATURDAY MORNING, my husband went in to work. As an engineer, he is much busier than I am.

I tidied up the house after breakfast. Seeing my son, Dongdong, hadn't woken up, I sat down to read for a while. Since I had the baby, I've learned to make use of every bit of my time.

Mom and Dad walked in one after another.

"Do you still work on weekends?" asked Mom.

"It's my side interest," said I.

"How about we talk when you're free?" said Dad.

"Mom and Dad, it's okay. Take a seat. Timewise, it all depends on yourself. That's the life here."

I can see they are restrained in living here, particularly

when my significant other is at home, although he is an affable person and is kind to them. In general, old people don't feel as comfortable in their kid's home as in their own.

I shut the book. Occupied during the week, I ought to spend more time with the parents on weekends.

My mother said, "Every time I come to America, the most prominent feeling is loneliness. I don't see many people around while going out and can get nervous after a while."

I said, "Yeah, I've been here so long, and I'm still not accustomed to it. Especially after staying at home for a long period, I feel isolated from the world. That's the reason many old people in the States don't dare to retire when they reach retirement age, since they don't have enough money, or they fear dejection."

"How old can you retire in America?" asked my father.

"Based on your Social Security pension, at present, both men and women are the same at sixty-six. It may get pushed out further. I don't know if I can get it for my age."

My mother glared and said, "Do you really need to put it off for that long? Don't ladies retire at fifty-five and men at sixty in China? America is the richest place on the planet. How could that be?"

I said, "These things are complicated. Each nation's circumstance is different." I'd prefer not to talk excessively. It's a big subject. If I extend it, they'd say coming to America was the wrong decision. I know they really want us to go back to China, as they've been here several times and haven't liked it.

My dad said, "We have little activity here every day except to take care of Dongdong and do chores."

"The key is we can't go anyplace without driving," my mother said. "Unlike at home, where the buses and subways run all over the place, and you can hop on them to get anywhere. Besides, it's free for elderly."

My dad took a sympathetic look at my mother and said, "It's silent here on weekdays. Whenever a car passes by, your mother turns and looks out the window. When you get off work, you'll be all busy again. There's not much time to sit together and talk. We feel lonely after a while."

Hearing these words, I felt a sense of guilt in my heart and hurriedly said, "I'm sorry. We are both too busy these days to consider your feelings. I'll always show you around when I have time on the weekends."

My mother said, "There's little to see. Everyone is sitting in an iron-clad car when they go out. You can't see anyone on the road, except for a few people in the shops. Unlike China, where the streets are full of people. Just standing by the roadside watching people is a pastime."

My mother is right. A reasonable person would feel this way.

My dad asked, "Then how do you go out when you're old?"

"Drive yourself."

"What about at eighty years old?"

"Drive yourself if you want to go out."

I told them about an experience I had a few years ago. It was drizzling, and the road was slippery that day. I'm a cautious driver. When I arrived at the intersection, I met a yellow light and braked. Just as the car stopped, there was a loud "bang," and my car was rear-ended. The vehicle swayed by and moved a few steps forward. Luckily, I didn't have a car in front of me; otherwise, I'd be sandwiched. Looking back, I saw it was a large American car that had hit me from behind. I got out of the car and stood there waiting for the driver to come out. As I was pondering, the door opened slowly, and a crutch quivered under it. I saw an old white man, at least eighty years old, trying hard to get up from his seat, but he failed twice. I hurried over to give him a hand. He grabbed my hand and implored, "I can provide you with cash to settle this in private. Please don't tell the insurance company. If they know I had another accident, I can't drive out to buy groceries anymore." Hearing this, I was very sorry for him. Since there was not much damage to the car, I let him go. I've never forgotten the tears in his eyes as he thanked me.

My mother exhaled.

My dad looked at my mom and wanted to say something but stopped after she gave him a wink.

I said, "Dad, if you have anything to say, just say it. Do you want me to learn the computer again?"

He said, "Not exactly. We wanted to say that the last time we came here, but you had just had the baby, so we didn't mention it. We mean"—he paused—"your mother and I feel your life is very austere, and the place you live is lonely. We hope you work harder and earn more money, so you could move to the city in the future."

Before I went to bed at night, I told my husband what my father had said. He laughed so hard he couldn't stand up. He was interested in how I answered my father. What can I say? It's not just that America is a big land, everybody has a car, the suburban villas are spacious and comfortable with our own yards and garages, the schools are better, and the crime rate is low. My husband said, "Your summary is comprehensive. Well, all you have to do is tell them we're rich and we live in a big American *haozi*"—a Chinese word that means *mouse* but sounds like the English word *house*.

I glared at him and said, "Do you think they'll believe it?"

Hearing us talking about the big mouse, Dongdong, who was sitting on his little bed, giggled and kept repeating, "Big mouse, big mouse." He was born in the year of mouse and has a heap of mouse toys close by.

The big "haozi" we bought is brand-new. My husband and I watched the workers build this house. One weekend, we sat on the construction site and observed for two hours straight. We were stunned to see how fast it went up, like heaping up building blocks. Only a few nails were hammered on the thin strips of wood that intersected. They started from nothing on the foundation early in the day, and by the night the whole house frame was put up. My husband asked me, "Do you dare to live here with so many tornadoes in America?"

"No!" I replied decidedly. "But we've put down the deposit. Where do we live if we give this one up?"

This is how all houses are built throughout the United

States. The interior is covered by drywall made of gypsum and paper that can be punched through with a fist while the exterior is covered with vinyl siding. An upgraded exterior version would be pasted with a thin layer of plaster or "face bricks." Coming back a few decades later, you'd see a declining or run-down neighborhood. A while back, my husband showed me a photo of a colleague's house. A large area of decorative stones attached to the front of the house had crumbled into a wreck.

That's part of the fast-food economy. Such a house also has a name: "McMansion." My husband often said we'd bought a fake mansion for a price of a real mansion. What a joke!

Since my husband didn't have to work this weekend, we took my mom and dad to a slightly upscale Italian restaurant. It wasn't too crowded, since we arrived early. We picked a quiet corner and sat down. Dongdong sat in a high chair for babies. Learning to speak at this age, he'd keep shouting, "Wa-wa," when he saw a stranger.

My husband put one of the menus handed out by the host in front of my parents.

My mother said with a little embarrassment, "You know I'm blind."

"Some dishes on the menu have pictures for your reference." My husband was enthusiastic. "Let me read it so you can choose."

The Italian diet doesn't have much variety—different

plates of pasta, pizza and salad dishes. My husband patiently described them one by one.

"Noodles?" My mom shook her head. "What's so great about noodles? I only eat noodles when I don't have time to cook. We come to the restaurant to eat noodles?"

"This is *Italian* noodles, also called spaghetti," my husband said. "The seasoning added isn't the same. They're the Western style."

"Well, then, try it," said Mom.

We ended up ordering a bit of everything.

Dongdong was sitting in his high chair and holding a piece of pizza in one hand. With the red tomato sauce all over his face, he was bobbing his head and humming while eating. Everyone else was quiet.

After a while, my husband tried to open the conversation and said, "Although our small family isn't rich, it's still affluent."

"We've come a few times, and we know it's difficult in America," my dad said. "Jobs aren't stable, and you retire so late. You should try to save more. Today's meal will probably cost a lot of money. To be honest, the pasta isn't as good as your mother's fried noodles."

My mother grinned and said, "It's delicious. It has a rich, creamy flavor. The old man is not used to Western food, so he talks nonsense." She added, "This reminds me of the Chinese restaurant we ate in when we came last time. Do you remember the twenty dollars you left on the table when we left? At the time, I whispered to your dad that it was a real bargain to eat at a restaurant in America. I told your aunt after we returned to China, and she laughed at me and said I'm as stupid as a pumpkin. Now I know the twenty dollars was only a tip."

We all laughed. Dongdong also patted two greasy little hands, shouting, "Wa-wa-wa."

After laughing, my father said to my husband seriously, "Last time I talked to Yiting and suggested she should study the computer. She's still young."

I'd always thought it was a casual idea and didn't expect him to be serious.

"I know you've loved literature since you were a child," my dad said. "I've always had a concern." He rubbed his thumb over his middle finger and forefinger and said, "Now this is called the success. You might think it's tacky, but that's what real life is all about. It is right to comply with social customs and wrong to contradict them. Who still reads these leisure books nowadays? Most people don't want to learn something they have little chance to use. The novels are all fabricated. What's there to read and write about?"

Silence fell.

Seeing the atmosphere was a little tense, my mother said in a hurry, "Your father was worried about you." Then she glanced at my husband.

I looked at them in astonishment. There must be a story behind those words. My current job hurts their deep-rooted vanity when they engage in dialogue and comparisons among relatives and friends.

My husband said, "Father is right. These days, society has become materialistic, and money is the hero. However, *the price we pay for material wealth shouldn't be spiritual poverty.*" He paused, and when my father said nothing, he added, "Don't stress too much over Yiting. Her novels are fascinating. Please read them when you're free. I envy her for having such a hobby and a job she likes. We have just enough money. It's fine."

I am grateful to my husband from the bottom of my heart. In fact, the vast majority of people in our time are painting tigers like cats, whether they're white or black.

I didn't join the conversation as I didn't want them to think I'm an unfilial daughter. However, I truly prefer not to live according to the desires of my elders; I don't regard filial piety and making my parents happy as the ultimate goal of my life.

When we left the restaurant, my mother quietly reminded me I had put no cash on the table. I said we were in a Chinese restaurant last time, so I was afraid the manager would pinch the server's tip. This time, I left a tip on the credit card.

ABOUT THE AUTHOR 关于作者

郑丽青，中国合肥人，大学毕业后从事建筑设计工作，1988年随先生来美国。过去三十年里，她做过各种各样的工作，从中餐馆，工厂，建筑事务所，学校，到高科技公司。在这期间，有机会接触到美国各个阶层的人，近距离地体会他们的喜怒哀乐，特别是生活在这里的华人。她的写作专注于描述和揭示她所感知的世界。本书是基于她在美国三十年生活经历的短篇小说集的第一部。她和先生王许成住在加州圣地亚哥。

A native of Hefei, China, Lynn (Liqing) Zheng worked as an architectural designer after college and came to the United States with her husband in 1988. Over the past thirty years, she's performed a wide variety of jobs, working in Chinese restaurants, factories, an architecture firm, a school and a high-tech company. Her diverse experiences have brought Lynn into contact with individuals from all walks of life in the United States, especially those in the Chinese community, and to experience their triumphs, struggles, and agonies at close quarters. Her writings are focused on depicting and revealing the world as she perceives it. This book, her first collection of short stories, is based on her thirty years of life in the United States. Lynn lives with her husband, Alex (Xucheng) Wang, in San Diego, California.

《错位: 生在中国，活在美国》是一部小说。名字、人物、事件和地点都是作者想象的产物或虚构的。任何与人、事件和地点的相似之处都完全是巧合。

版权所有 © 2018 郑丽青，王许成
作者保留所有权利。
未经作者书面许可，不得以任何形式或通过任何电子或机械手段复制本书的任何部分，包括信息存储和检索系统，除非在书评中使用简要引文。

"Dislocation: Born in China, Living in America" is a work of fiction. Names, characters, incidents, and places are the production of the author's imagination or used fictitiously. Any resemblance to persons, living or dead, incidents, and places is entirely coincidental.

Copyright © 2018 by Lynn (Liqing) Zheng and Alex (Xucheng) Wang
All rights reserved.
No part of this book may be reproduced in any form or by any electronic or mechanical means, including information storage and retrieval systems, without written permission from the author, except for the use of brief quotations in a book review.

ISBN 978-1-7327725-3-3

English Editing 英文编辑: Eliza Dee
Cover art 封面艺术：Yanli Wang
Book design 书籍设计: Alex Wang 王许成

Author website 作者网站: https://lynn-zheng.com
Email 电子邮件: lynnzhengstories@gmail.com

www.ingramcontent.com/pod-product-compliance
Lightning Source LLC
Chambersburg PA
CBHW031349040426
42444CB00005B/249